CANADA'S GUIDE TO WINE AND FOOD

VINES

third edition

Dedicated to Elle Anne Sendzik

Buyer's Guide to Canadian Wine

VINES

third edition

by Walter Sendzik and Christopher Waters

foreword by Ron MacLean

Vines Publishing

Visit our web site at www.vinesmag.com

Edited by Melanie Gerbes
Cover photograph by Paul Weeks

Printed and bound in Canada

National Library of Canada Cataloguing in Publication Data
Sendzik, Walter
    Vines buyer's guide to Canadian wines/Walter Sendzik
    and Christopher Waters.

    Includes index.
    ISBN 0-9734490

    1. Wine and wine making—Canada. 2. Wine and wine making —Canada—
Handbooks, manuals etc. I. Waters, Christopher. II. Title. III. Title: Buyer's guide to
Canadian wine.
TP559.C3S45 2002   641.2'2'0971   C2002-911065-3

**For a free copy of *Vines* magazine,
contact us at 1-888-883-3372.**

CONTENTS

FOREWORD

On September 1st, 1984 Cari and I got married. That
night we celebrated with a bottle of Stags Leap. We
signed, dated and kept the cork. We still collect corks.
A recent addition to the collection stems from a nice
dinner with Brian and Jennifer Burke in Vancouver. Brian's
the general manager of the National Hockey League's
Vancouver Canucks. They chose the wine – Sumac Ridge
Estates Pinnacle, a blend of Merlot, Cabernet Sauvignon
and Cabernet Franc. This 1998 was a blockbuster!

In our cork collection we have some other neat Canucks.
In the late seventies, while dating Cari, a favourite night was
spent with pizza and Sommet Rouge, a table wine from
Calona Vineyards. We grew up in Red Deer, Alberta, so B.C.
wines were a large part of our youth.

In 1986, we moved to Toronto where I began working
with Hockey Night in Canada. A life with Grapes! In those
early years in Ontario we were tourists and we were really
smitten with Niagara. The first winery we visited was
Hillebrand Estates. After our trip we shared a Muscat with
our new neighbours.

In 1989 we bought our first home in Ancaster. The Old
Mill restaurant was next door and we celebrated with the
most expensive wine on the menu, a $35 Cabernet from
Château des Charmes. We became very familiar with the
drive along Highway 20 atop the Niagara Escarpment and
its inherent charms. We enjoyed Riesling from Vineland
Estates, Chardonnay from Cave Springs Cellars, Laura's
Blend from Creekside Estates, and anything from De Sousa
Cellars in Beamsville.

Then it would be on to Niagara-on-the-Lake. Favourites there include, Inniskillin's Pinot Noir, Marynissen's Sauvignon Blanc, Pillitteri's Merlot, and the wines from Peller Estates. Every month we purchase two new bottles from Peller in a door-to-door program they offer. We have cases of Peller's past greats, like the 1998 Private Reserve Cabernet Sauvignon. Another spark that has caught our attention is Pinot Gris from Malivoire Wine Company. It has a ladybug on the label.

I am always grateful for the sound of a cork popping in the kitchen. For me, a perfect day off has to be a weekday. At around 4 p.m. out comes the cork, on goes the music. I really enjoy *Disc Drive* with Jurgen Gothe on CBC's Radio 2. Add to that a good book and of course, a snooze. One of the authors I really enjoy happens to be John Ralston Saul. *Voltaires Bastards* carried me through a wild contract negotiation in the fall of 2002. It essentially keys in on humanism and common sense. Saul has certainly done his part for Canadian wine. He transformed the cellar at Rideau Hall and makes all of the Governor-General's galas tastefully Canadian.

Speaking of tasteful Canadians, I'm grateful for Donald Ziraldo, co-founder of Inniskillin Wines. A couple of years ago Donald invited Cari and me to experience the Icewine harvest and Niagara Icewine Festival held every year in late January. Canada has given the world hockey, but if you're looking for the ultimate gift to export, it's Icewine.

The NHL has certainly embraced the nectar. Mario Lemieux has an entire wall of '66 Château Petrus. Wayne Gretzky is a fan as well, but just as Wayne manufactured greatness out of any set of wingers, he makes an occasion out of any label. As long as they don't take the red line out of winemaking!

In your hands you hold the opener to a wonderful night with Canadian wines. Walter Sendzik and Vines Magazine are friends and mentors to our appreciation of Canada's best.

Go Canucks!

Ron MacLean
Toronto

ACKNOWLEDGMENTS

First, thanks go to the entire panel who graciously donated their time to taste a lot of wine. To Jason Alikakos, Derek Barnett, Linda Bramble, Laurie Clark, Candace Collins, Ray Cornell, Roberto DiDomenico, Fred Gamula, Tim Kerr, Cari MacLean, Brett Marshall, Ken Mowat, Steven Page, Victor Page, Angelo Pavan, Thomas Pennachetti, Rod Phillips, Gary Pickering, Carolyn Ricketts, George Ricketts, Del Rollo, Brian Schmidt, Tom Seaver, Matthew Speck, Ilia Suter, Anna Weiss, Joe Will and Kara Willie for all of the comments, notes and general discussions about the wine. Without your valuable input, this book would be a shell of what it is.

To Ron MacLean for writing the foreword to this book. Thank you for sharing your time and talent to help with the tasting of wines for the book.

To Bremner Biscuit Company from Denver, Colorado, the official cracker of the *Vines* tasting panel, for continued support of our efforts. Our purple-tongued tasters salute you!

To Vintage Niagara Adventures and Tammy Kruk for providing bottle wraps for all the tastings. VNA ensured all tastings were indeed blind with their easy-to-use adhesive wrappers. Visit www.vna.on.ca for more information on their range of quality wine accessories.

To all those who have supported the idea that a book like this could be published annually—to Kara Wille, Pat Waters, Melanie Sendzik, Mom and Dad Sendzik and the rest of the Sendzik and Waters clan, we extend a big hug and thanks for putting up with all those weekends spent tasting wine and those endlessly long nights writing this book. (An extra special thanks to Melanie for putting up with the untold number of bottles that clutter the kitchen, basement, hallway and living room of 159 York Street.)

Also to Ali and Scully, who missed out on numerous walks and visits to the park. You now have your masters' undivided attention. Look out squirrels, here we come.

Finally, and most importantly, we would like to acknowledge those in the Canadian wine industry who have supported *Vines Magazine* since our earliest days. *Vines* is an offshoot of your years of hard work. If it were not for the great number of hardworking winemakers and entrepreneurs who have taken the Canadian wine industry to new heights, this book could not have been completed. This buyer's guide is testimony to your tireless efforts to make great wine.

By purchasing this book, you show your support of products that are 100 per cent Canadian. Consider buying another copy; it would make a great stocking stuffer or birthday gift for the wine enthusiasts on your list.

INTRODUCTION

A funny thing happens when you taste through 1,300 or more wines: an unerring picture of quality comes into focus. In the weeks and months of panel tastings for the third edition of this buyer's guide, we tasted every major and emerging varietal and style produced in Ontario and British Columbia for a snapshot of how the homegrown character of each is developing.

Canadian wine has never been better. And it's getting better all the time.

Wine tells us something new with every vintage. The life-enhancing drink is a reflection of its growing region's unique climate, soil, location and weather conditions, which all impact on the flavours and quality of the finished product.

Canadian wine tells how imagination and commitment have laid the groundwork for wine regions every bit as good as any the rest of the world has to offer. Ontario and British Columbia at their best rival Napa, Burgundy or Bordeaux.

Looking back, we note that it has been only in the past twenty-five years that winemakers began to focus on producing quality, European-styled, vinifera wines. Sure, back in the 1960s and 1970s, Canadian wineries produced blended table wine and a lot of "pop" wines, which sold very well, but a shift took place in the Canadian wine industry in the mid 1970s that revolutionized the quality of the wines.

Led by mavericks such as Karl Kaiser and Donald Ziraldo (who opened Inniskillin, Canada's first estate winery in 1975), Paul Bosc Sr. of Château des Charmes and Joe Pohorly, founder of Newark Winery (which would become Hillebrand Estates Winery after he sold it), the industry started to focus on producing varietal wines from French hybrid and European vinifera grapes. In British Columbia, the pioneering spirit was furthered by Harry McWatters of Sumac Ridge Estate Winery, George Heiss of Gray Monk Cellars and Bob and Lee Claremont, who opened the first estate winery in British Columbia—the now-defunct Claremont—in 1979.

These visionaries had the nerve and the commitment to challenge the status quo. Although many doubted their collective belief that classic vinifera vines such as Chardonnay, Riesling, Cabernet Franc and Merlot could be successfully planted in certain areas of Canada, these pioneers went out and proved that Canada could sustain and produce quality grapes, especially in Niagara and the Okanagan Valley. These were planted along with French hybrids such as Vidal, Baco Noir and Maréchal Foch, and by the early 1980s, a small number of wineries were crafting surprisingly well-made wines.

After it was demonstrated that the fertile soils and climate conditions of southern Ontario and the Okanagan Valley could yield consistent vinifera wines, a second wave of winemakers emerged in the 1980s. Producers such as Colio Wines, Cave Spring Cellars, Pelee Island Winery, Reif Estate Winery and Vineland Estates in Ontario and Calona Wines, Gehringer Brothers and Quails' Gate in British Columbia gave the fledgling industry an extra boost.

These vintners went on to inspire a wave of quality-minded wineries. Some of these include amateur-turned-pro operations Marynissen Estates and Lakeview Cellars in Niagara, as well as farm-gate producers Henry of Pelham Family Estate and Pillitteri Estates in Niagara and Blue Mountain Vineyard and Cellars, St. Hubertus Vineyard and Wild Goose Vineyards in the Okanagan Valley.

Much of the activity in the late 1980s and early 1990s was inspired by NAFTA (the North American Free Trade Agreement), as well as the founding of the Vintners Quality Alliance, first in Ontario in 1989, then in British Columbia in 1990. The spectre of a flood of bulk jug wine from California pouring into Canada led domestic wineries to ratchet up the quality of the wine they were producing so they could establish their own niche at the nation's liquor stores.

Instituting winemaking standards through the VQA, which represents the best Canada has to offer in the way of domestic wine, helped achieve that goal. It was a pivotal move taken by the industry to ensure the quality of the wines being produced. It brought the wineries in British Columbia and Ontario together, working to promote Canadian wines at a time when most people didn't believe in them. Many quality-minded wineries operating outside of the VQA also focus their production on 100 per cent product-of-Canada wines.

The latest surge is a wave of super-premium producers, wineries such as Burrowing Owl Vineyards, CedarCreek Estate Winery and Paradise Ranch Winery in British Columbia and Creekside Estate, Daniel Lenko Estate Winery, The Malivoire Wine Company, Thirty Bench Vineyard and Thirteenth Street Wine Company in Niagara. All are looking to hit a high note with quality vintages made with low yields of carefully farmed fruit.

With Canadian wineries routinely bringing home top awards from international competitions, the quality of domestic wine has never been better. Unfortunately, consumer support for Canadian wine across the country hasn't kept pace. Certainly Icewine is always going to be the specialty item that carries the banner for Canadian wineries into the international arena, but there's more to the industry than sweet dessert wines. Canadian table wines are snapping up medals at VinItaly, the International Wine and Spirit Competition in London, England, and other prestigious world-class wine events. Our reds are beginning to stand shoulder-to-shoulder with well-known reds from California, Australia and Europe. And yet, consumers are still reluctant to buy Canadian wines.

That's where this book can help. We designed this third edition to make it easier for consumers to find, learn about and buy Canadian wines. We've arranged the wines by grape variety or style. If you're a fan of Chardonnay, for example, the Chardonnay section will give you general information about the varietal and how it's produced in Canada. We follow this with an exhaustive review section on Chardonnays made by Canadian wineries, starting with the best in the nation and ranking the wines from "Highly Recommended" to "Recommended" to "Quite Good." The same format applies to all widely planted grape varieties. In the case of lesser-known varieties, they have been grouped together for your convenience.

After tasting the broad range of wines produced in Ontario and British Columbia, we were reminded of the wonderful experience—the wide range of tastes and flavours—that only wine can bring to the senses. There's nothing faddish about great wine. It stimulates passions and emotions. It makes memories. It evokes a certain wow factor.

Many have said that Canadian wines are one of our best-kept secrets, but we feel it's time to spread the word. Wine is best enjoyed with family and friends. By highlighting these exciting bottles, we welcome you to join in the celebration.

About *Vines* Magazine

Vines is Canada's only truly national wine magazine. It grew out of our conviction that there was an audience for a magazine that explored and celebrated the good life of wine. Our belief is that the appreciation of wine is part of a multidimensional lifestyle. People who drink wine also lead active lives and have a wide variety of other interests, so why should we place wine in a vacuum, isolated from everything else that stimulates and enriches our lives?

We wanted to put something on the newsstands that makes it clear to you that we understand and respect your approach to wine, your knowledge of it and your broad range of experiences with it.

For the past six years we have been providing readers with a magazine that transcends the staid, pretentious view of wine upheld by other wine publications. We were the first wine magazine in Canada to view wine as part of a lifestyle, not as a hobby or an elite club. Readers have come to understand that, with *Vines*, their interest in wine is encouraged to develop through personal experimentation. They are appreciated for their level of wine knowledge, not lectured on it. It's a small, but very significant point.

We believed that casual consumers who enjoy a glass of wine would pick up a wine magazine without feeling intimidated if the publication spoke to them. It was an idea that wine writing can be both entertaining and educational. By placing wine in a cultural context, which includes music, food, art, literature and so much more, we have given readers a larger forum from which they can build their own personal experiences with wine.

And the key element in this tale of a dream reaching fruition is the people behind the conviction. We're not wine snobs—you can trust me on that one. We love wine for what it is: a work of art that conveys stories on so many different levels. For more information on *Vines Magazine*, visit our web site at www.vinesmag.com.

How Were the Reviews Created?

A collective of people created the reviews for the buyer's guide. The process started back in February 2003 when a fax was sent to all the wineries in British Columbia and Ontario. The request was for wineries to submit wines available to the consumer through 2003-04 — whether at liquor stores or through wine shops and boutiques. The stipulation was that the wine must be VQA certified and/or use 100 per cent grown-in-Canada grapes. Within weeks, the *Vines* office was flooded with cases of wine. The boxes took over an entire floor of our St. Catharines operation. Once all the wines were entered into our database—more than 1,300 were submitted this year—we divided up the varieties and began the long process of organizing the panel tastings. Recognizing that everyone has a different palate, we wanted to have diverse panels with different members to fully explore the wines each time. Panels consisted of four to six people. Walter Sendzik and Christopher Waters, two of Canada's leading wine experts, were the regulars, with winemakers, wine educators, sommeliers, wine enthusiasts and wine consumers rounding out the panel.

Within their respective groups, we divided the wines by vintage and then by reserve and and other meaningful classifications. All tastings were done blind, which means that the panel members only knew the wine type, but not the producer or the region where it was produced. This allowed for the greatest amount of objectivity. Each panel member was directed to score the wines based on the *Vines Magazine* five-star rating system. They were also asked to give detailed descriptions of the wine. At the end of each tasting, we collected the tasting sheets and compiled the scores and accorded each wine its ranking.

The difference between reviews in this buyer's guide and others written by wine critics is that these are much more accurate, being based on a collective resource of information versus the opinions and peccadilloes of just one person.

And finally, Walter Sendzik and Christopher Waters wrote all the reviews. We approached each review with the consumer in mind. Our goal was to educate and entertain. The reviews are a reflection of the wine—the higher the ranking, the more verbose the review. And wines are also a part of our culture—we know you'll be able to relate to our cultural references.

Who Are the Reviewers?

Jason Alikakos, Proprietor, Jonathans of Oakville

Derek Barnett, winemaker, Lailey Vineyards, Niagara-on-the-Lake

Dr. Linda Bramble, sommelier, wine writer, educator and industry liaison for the Cool Climate Oenology and Viticulture Institute, Brock University, St. Catharines

Laurie Clark, wine enthusiast, Toronto

Candace Collins, wine enthusiast, Toronto

Ray Cornell, winemaker, Harvest Estates Wines and Hernder Estates Winery, St. Catharines

Roberto DiDomenico, winemaker, Reif Estate Winery, Niagara-on-the-Lake

Fred Gamula, chief sommelier of Vintage Inns, Niagara-on-the-Lake

Cari MacLean, wine enthusiast, Toronto

Ron MacLean, wine enthusiast, Toronto

Brett Marshall, Trinchero Family Estates, California

Ken Mowat, winemaker Harbour Estates Winery, Jordan

Tim Kerr, sommelier, New York City

Steven Page, Barenaked Ladies lead singer and wine lover, Toronto

Victor Page, wine enthusiast, Toronto

Angelo Pavan, winemaker, Cave Spring Cellars, Jordan

Thomas Pennachetti, Cave Spring Cellars, Jordan

Dr. Rod Phillips, *Ottawa Citizen* wine writer, senior editor *Vines* magazine, sommelier, director of the National Capital Sommelier Guild and author of *A Short History of Wine* (Penguin UK, 2000), Ottawa

Dr. Gary Pickering, oenologist and sensory scientist, Cool Climate Oenology and Viticulture Institute, Brock University, St. Catharines

Del Rollo, sommelier, Manager of Hospitality Relations, Jackson-Triggs Niagara Estate Winery, NOTL

Carolyn Ricketts, wine enthusiast, Toronto

George Ricketts, wine enthusiast, Toronto

Brian Schmidt, winemaker, Vineland Estates Winery, Vineland

Tom Seaver, winemaker, Jackson-Triggs Niagara Estate Winery, Niagara-on-the-Lake

Walter Sendzik, publisher/editor of *Vines* magazine, co-author of the *Vines Buyer's Guide to Canadian Wine*, St. Catharines

Steven Sokolowski, wine collector, Toronto

Matthew Speck, vice president/viticulturalist, Henry of Pelham Family Estate Winery, St. Catharines

Ilia Suter, assistant winemaker, Cave Spring Cellars, Jordan

Christopher Waters, managing editor of *Vines* magazine, co-author of the *Vines Buyer's Guide to Canadian Wine*, wine columnist for the *St. Catharines Standard*

Anna Weiss, grape grower, St. Catharines

Joe Will, winemaker and owner, Strewn Wines Inc., Niagara-on-the-Lake

The *Vines* Magazine Rating System

Our rating is based on a five-star system. A score is given only after a thorough, objective assessment of the wine's qualities. After each panelist submits a rating for the wine, the ratings are aggregated and the wine is awarded a ranking within the five-star system.

Vines Award *****

To achieve this ranking the wine must be of outstanding quality. The panel awards this mark if the wine is the best of the tasting. In some cases, the panel has decided that the top wines did not reach the level of superlative quality and therefore some sections in the book will not have a *Vines* Award.

Highly Recommended ****

For a wine to achieve this ranking it must be a truly exceptional example of its grape variety.

Recommended ***

These are wines that have positive characteristics that were singled out by our panel.

Quite Good **

All are good, quaffable wines.

Acceptable *

Decent wine, free of faults. This category of faint-praise reviews, used in *Vines* magazine, is omitted in this book to save space for showcasing only the finest wines produced in Canada.

Note: Wines that were deemed faulted or not suitable for recommendation in a buyer's guide were not reviewed.

How to Read the Reviews

This is the ranking category

Winery

Vintage and proper
name of wine

Appellation recognized
by the VQA

VINES AWARD

Mission Hill Family Estate Winery
1999 Merlot Reserve
Okanagan Valley VQA $24 (496109)
When the panel tasted Mission Hill's 1999 Merlot,
it was hard for them to believe it indeed came
from a Canadian producer. Lush notes of blueberry and vanilla filled the glass. Wonderful
flavours of blueberry, blackcurrant and hints of
pine and cedar illustrate its complexity. Warm,
soft and supple, this Merlot has it all.

Vintners Quality Alliance

Price of wine based on
the province of origin.
Prices will vary based
on province, on-line
stores, and at the
winery

CSPU number (If a
wine does not have a
number, it means it is
sold only at the winery)

CANADIAN WINE REGIONS

British Columbia

British Columbia has four grape growing regions that are recognized as viticultural areas by VQA Canada. The largest of the four is the **Okanagan Valley**, in the central southern part of British Columbia, nestled in the Cascade Mountain Range that runs through into Washington State. Nearby is a much smaller viticultural area, the **Similkameen Valley**. The other two viticultural areas are the **Fraser Valley** and **Vancouver Island**, which are both considered coastal regions.

According to the British Columbia Wine Institute, the province has more than 5,000 acres of vineyards dedicated to wine production. There are more than 70 wineries in British Columbia, although most are farmgate companies that produce only small amounts of wine.

Similar to Ontario's history of wine production, British Columbia's started back in the 1930s with plantings of Labrusca varieties such as Concord, Niagara, Patricia, Sheridan and Bath. Although the Okanagan Valley was a natural site for vineyard development since apple orchards flourished in the area, it was Growers' Wine Company and Victoria Wineries located on Vancouver Island that, as early as 1930, first produced wines from the local Labrusca grapes. The Okanagan's oldest winery, Calona Wines, was established in 1936.

Concentrated vineyard development took hold in the 1960s when the B.C. government encouraged the planting of vines by passing a law that stated wines made in the province had to contain a minimum of 25 per cent B.C. grown grapes. Andrew Peller, a pioneer in the Canadian wine industry, built Andrés Wines in 1961 in Port Moody. Other wineries opened and closed, among them the first incarnation of Mission Hill Winery.

Just as the first car ever built wasn't a Cadillac or Corvette, the wines produced during the early years of B.C.'s modern wine history were not palate pleasers. Created from French and American hybrids such as De Chaunac, Maréchal Foch, Verdelet, Baco Noir and Okanagan Riesling, the wines were palatable, but not exactly noble in comparison to classic vinifera wines from the Old World. But the mini-boom, started with the support of the B.C. government and entrepreneurial minds of people such as Peller, led farmers to turn orchards into vineyards, creating an environment that would eventually lead to experimentation with vinifera varieties.

By the late 1970s, the B.C. government once again stepped in to help the wine industry. Wineries were permitted to open on-site retail stores and grants were provided to allow farmers to experiment with other grape varieties such as Pinot Blanc, Gewürztraminer and Ehrenfelser. As well, provincial legislation was introduced that created estate wineries. The law stipulated that estate or cottage wineries had to own 20 acres of vineyard, could only produce up to 30,000 gallons of wine and had to use 100 per cent grapes from British Columbia, of which 50 per cent had to come from the estate. The first estate winery to open under the new act was Claremont in 1979.

The 1980s saw an influx of small estate wineries that took advantage of the provincial government's support. Early farmgate winery pioneers such as Sumac Ridge and Gray Monk and entrepreneurs such as Anthony von Mandl, who purchased a dilapidated winery in 1981 once known as — and eventually renamed — Mission Hill, led the charge to build a modern wine industry in British Columbia.

As in Ontario, the North American Free Trade Agreement in 1988 had an enormous impact on the grape growing industry in British Columbia. Growers were paid by the federal government to rip out Labrusca and French hybrid grapes and plant vinifera whites such as Riesling, Gewürztraminer, Chardonnay, Pinot Blanc, Pinot Gris, and red vinifera such as Pinot Noir, Merlot, and Cabernet Sauvignon. The program was aimed at increasing the quality of grapes to help offset the flood of bulk wine that was feared would pour into Canada once the trade barriers were removed. Although resisted in the beginning by growers, NAFTA proved to be a key in getting the Canadian wine industry to the next level.

Since the early 1990s, with the year-over-year increase in vinifera wines from British Columbia, the industry has truly taken off. Thanks to the support from B.C. consumers and restaurants, which is not the case in the fickle Ontario market, wineries in British Columbia have established a strong presence in the Pacific Northwest. Wineries such as Calona Wines with talented winemaker Howard Soon, Mission Hill Family Estate Winery with its New Zealand-born winemaker John Simes and Jackson-Triggs Okanagan Estate Winery's winemaker Bruce Nicholson, are all creating wines that have taken home major international awards. And medium-sized wineries such as Quails' Gate Estate Winery, Burrowing Owl Estate Winery and Tinhorn Creek Estate Winery have become stalwarts in creating consistently high-end, quality wines. With the supporting cast of farmgate wineries such as Hester Creek Winery, Hillside Estates, Lake Breeze Winery and La Frenz Winery, which are intent on making small-batch, premium wines, the reputation of British Columbia wineries as producers of excellent wine is quickly growing on the international stage.

The biggest question that needs to be answered, both in British Columbia and Ontario, is which grape produces most consistently in making great wines? Considering that 95 per cent of the grape production in British Columbia comes from the Okanagan Valley, it's the best place to look at how well certain grapes perform. Since 1998, when we started producing our guides to Canadian wines, we have noted the best-performing wines each year. Based on the results of our tastings and interviews with winemakers, it's clear that the northern part of the Okanagan Valley, from Summerland and up, is better suited for whites such as Chardonnay, Gewürztraminer, Sauvignon Blanc, Pinot Blanc and Pinot Gris. The growing season can be as much as two to three weeks earlier between this area and the southern part of the valley. Although arid by nature, the entire valley uses irrigation in creating ideal conditions for the grapes.

The southern part of the Okanagan Valley, a short 19-kilometre stretch from Oliver to Osoyoos, bordering

Washington State, is home to Canada's only desert, and the conditions are hot. A longer growing season in this area produces highly concentrated reds such as Merlot, Cabernet Sauvignon, and Pinot Noir. Over the past few years, wineries have scooped up most of the remaining land in the south and it's now a hot spot for vineyard development. Wine giants such as Jackson-Triggs and Mission Hill have invested heavily in the area. With controlled irrigation and aging vines, the level of quality red wines being produced has taken off.

Merlot, which is the most widely planted red in B.C., is definitely a wine to watch from British Columbia, as is Cabernet Sauvignon and Cabernet blends. Syrah and Shiraz — the jury's still out on what to label this well-spiced red wine — are yielding some impressive results, though on a smaller scale. Newly-planted Syrah vines will start to produce significant amounts of wine in the next two to three years.

Pinot Gris and Chardonnay are currently wrestling for supremacy amongst the white wine varietals. The best examples of both are made in a clean and fresh style that knows how to behave at the dinner table. And don't forget Icewine. Although not as well known around the world as Ontario is for its Icewine, British Columbia's Okanagan Valley has the potential every year to produce it. An arctic blast in December or January usually allows for the perfect conditions. Pinot Blanc, Ehrenfelser and Chardonnay Icewine are starting to establish a niche market, and even Pinot Noir Icewine was made in 2000 by Calona Wines.

The future looks bright for British Columbia's wine industry. With continued investment from the industry, a constant drive from the winemakers to produce better wines every year and continued support from consumers, B.C. wines will make a significant impression on the global wine scene soon.

Okanagan Valley

The Okanagan Valley, nestled in the Cascade Mountains, produces close to 95 per cent of British Columbia wines. Historically, the Okanagan Valley has been known as a fruit orchard belt, with apples, cherries and peaches as the staple products. Over the past two decades, grape growers and wineries have established grapes as a leading product of the area. Home to 70 wineries and 222 grape growers, it has 5,000 acres under vines. Dry, hot summer conditions are tempered by irrigation from the immense Okanagan Lake.

Similkameen Valley

An offshoot of the Okanagan, located over a mountain range west of the southern Okanagan Valley, the Similkameen Valley is home to a handful of wineries. Desert-like conditions are relieved by irrigation from the Similkameen River. This area has yet to establish itself as a major player.

Fraser Valley

The grape-growing region closest to Greater Vancouver, the Fraser Valley has been growing grapes since the 1960s. It is not overly populated with wineries, with only three in the area, but it is home to Andrés Wines in Port Moody.

Vancouver Island

The most westerly-designated grape growing region in Canada, Vancouver Island has revived its winemaking past. With 14 wineries situated on the Island, it appears there's enough confidence to make wine in this more humid and wet growing season. All the wineries are small estate companies that barely produce enough to satisfy more than the local restaurants. The results are varied and the jury is still out as to how well these wineries can make the wine and if they will ever be more than just small players in the industry.

For more information on British Columbia's wine industry check out www.winebc.com.

Ontario

Prior to the War of 1812, a retired German soldier grew grapes and made wine from Labrusca grapes on a plot of land near Mississauga. Corporal Johann Schiller stands as Ontario's winemaking pioneer, though it would be more than 50 years before a commercial operation hung out its shingle.

The first commercial winery in Canada was established on Pelee Island, which is located in Lake Erie, in 1866. The remains of the building, Vin Villa, still stand today, not far from the flourishing Pelee Island Winery. Pelee Island Winery has a string of retail shops, is the best selling VQA producer in the LCBO and has an expansive web site that accepts online orders. One wonders exactly how expansive a market Vin Villa had in its day.

Winery development flourished from the last 1800s to the early 1900s, with as many as 40 wineries in operation across the province. The industry continued to develop, even through Prohibition (1916-1927), as The Canadian Temperance Act allowed for the sale of wine, the only alcohol to be sold legally. An active bootleg trade between the border cities also meant Ontario wineries enjoyed strong, if illegal, sales to our American cousins.

Adhemar de Chaunac, who planted 40 different European grape varieties, including Chardonnay and Pinot Noir in Niagara Peninsula, conducted the first experimentation with grapes other than the native Labrusca varieties in 1946. The results were mixed to say the least. As late as the 1970s growers who invested in vineyards planted to Chardonnay, Riesling, Pinot Noir and other of the so-called "noble" vinifera grape varieties were considered by some to be foolhardy. We know better, and many of those early vineyards are the source for the Old Vines Chardonnay and Old Vines Merlot bottlings that are featured in some wineries reserve portfolios.

The chief output of Ontario's wineries was a wide variety of blended wines, often labeled as "ports" and "sherries." They were high in sugar and alcohol content — "three fights in every bottle" recalls my grandfather; lower-alcohol/drier wines gained popularity in the '60s and '70s.

The spark of transformation occurred in 1975 when Inniskillin was granted the first estate winery license in Ontario since Prohibition. A number of estate wineries followed in its wake, including Pelee Island Winery and Colio Estates Wines, located in what would be designated as the Lake Erie North Shore viticultural area.

The inception of the Free Trade Agreement with the United States in 1988 resulted in a rapid transformation of the province's vineyards, as two-thirds of the acreage planted with Labrusca grapes are ripped out and replanted with vinifera and French hybrid grape varieties. Even then suspicion of the long-term viability of vinifera grapes, such as Chardonnay, Pinot Noir, Merlot and Gewürztraminer, led to widescale planting of Vidal, Seyval Blanc, Maréchal Foch and Baco Noir.

A year later, the Vintners Quality Alliance (VQA) was created with 18 founding members. The alliance created a province-wide appellation system that detailed production and quality standards and regulations for winemaking. The system designated three viticultural areas: Niagara Peninsula, the area surrounding the southern tip of Lake Ontario which accounts for 80 per cent of the country's growing volume, Lake Erie North Shore and Pelee Island.

A decade later, when the VQA Act was proclaimed into law in Ontario, there were 52 VQA producing wineries. The act cemented the quality regulations and, best of all for consumers, created an enforcement arm that oversees comprehensive audits and periodic reviews of products available at winery retail stores, LCBO outlets and at licencees. Producers are accountable that their wines live up to VQA standards.

The growth of wineries continues at a rapid rate. There are more than 90 winery licenses issued in Ontario including cottage fruit wineries. Meanwhile acreage for wine grapes in Ontario amounts to more than 17,000 acres. Chardonnay remains the most popular single varietal followed by Riesling and Cabernet Franc. New varieties, such as Syrah, Viognier and Chenin Blanc, are coming on stream. One wonders what Ontario's vine census will look like 10 and 20 years down the line.

The VQA is currently working on the potential of naming sub-appellations within the three existing designated viticultural areas, looking at growing regions that reflect unique characteristics of its area, with likely candidates being the Beamsville Bench and the Niagara-on-the-Lake plains. Meanwhile, the vinous pioneers working at establishing a new designated viticultural area in Prince Edward County have their work cut out for them living up to hype created by early press reports claiming the area will overtake Niagara as Ontario's premium wine region. Bold words considering the small amount of wine produced from locally grown fruit.

If this talk of behind-the-scenes administration of the VQA leaves you cold (and you'd be forgiven for stifling a yawn at the mention of sub-appellations and other industry machinations), steel your determination with the fact that the VQA represents the future of the Canadian wine industry. Created in Ontario and adopted by British Columbia, it has established the framework for the growth and development of quality winemaking in Canada.

And the future looks bright, both at home and on the international front. Niagara's industry has benefited from recently announced Franco-Canadian joint-ventures, including Le Clos Jordan, an impressive start-up created by the country's largest wine company Vincor International and the Boisset Family of Burgundy dedicated to creating world-class Pinot Noir and Chardonnay. Canadian-born architectural visionary Frank Gehry has been commissioned to build the winery, which will focus even greater international attention on

Ontario and its winemaking capabilities. The first wines were made from the 2003 vintage.

There's also exciting news with a growing trend towards protecting our precious agricultural lands from ever-present threats of urban sprawl and development. A change in provincial government will hopefully bring much needed — long overdue, in our minds — leadership on this issue.

As we stated in the introduction, Canadian wine has never been better. And, it's getting better all the time. The province was blessed with a stellar harvest in 2002, which yielded impressive wines from bone dry to Icewine sweet. The early releases are recorded here. A large number of wines are still being babied by the producers and will hit liquor store shelves soon.

Agricultural industries are used to taking the good with the bad, as we go to press the prospects for 2003 vintage aren't as cheery. It has been a challenging growing season, particularly due to losses due to winter damage. The total effect won't be known until all of the grapes are in, but it seems certain the harvest will produce lower yields than usual.

To truly understand the Canadian wine industry, you have to taste the wines. There's plenty to try. Read on and we'll help you narrow your focus somewhat.

For more information about Ontario wines check out www.wineroute.com.

WHITE WINE

CHARDONNAY

In the world of wine, Chardonnay remains king. Although waning, its popularity is still such that most wine drinkers think white wine is synonymous with Chardonnay. What's puzzling about its great appeal, however, is that few consumers know what Chardonnay's actual flavour is because the wine is made in such a wide range of styles. Perhaps the root of its allure is its French-bred sophistication; perhaps it is simply that mass-produced Chardonnay is an easy-drinking wine that's smooth and generally straightforward.

The varietal has broad consumer appeal because of its complex aromas, distinctive flavours, rich mouth feel, and food-friendly nature. As a result of its popularity, plantings in North America now exceed those in France.

Chardonnay has taken its share of knocks, particularly from the ABC (Anything But Chardonnay) contingent of consumers who decried it as being as appetizing as being

FOOD PAIRING SUGGESTIONS
What goes with Chardonnay? What doesn't is more the question. With its relatively high acids, full-bodied nature and incredible versatility it can be enjoyed alone or with a wide variety of flavourful dishes. Considering the range of styles, there's an equally broad range of potential matches for the wines. Lighter wines are generally more food friendly, while some of the heavier oaked wines require more robust meals to balance the weight and concentrated flavours of the wine. Try dry and delicate sur lie wines with oysters and shellfish. Bigger wines can muscle in on salmon, roast chicken, and veal with cream sauces or earthy mushrooms

thwacked in the head with a two-by-four. The description is an apt one. New World Chardonnay producers went a little overboard with oak aging and other winemaking techniques in a "go big or go home" bout of one-up-manship.

We're happy to announce those days are over, and boldly predict Chardonnay's renaissance is here. The Vines panel spent three days tasting through the 16 cases of Chardonnay submitted and were uniformly impressed by the across-the-board quality of the wines. The days of over-oaked, over-amped Chardonnay are behind us, as winemakers have learned to listen to the vineyard and let the fruit speak to them. Balance is the goal these days.

The easy-to-produce, easy-to-enjoy white is a delight for all parties concerned — grape grower, winemaker, and consumer. The vines flourish in early spring, giving the early ripening variety a head start throughout the growing season.

Once in the winery, Chardonnay's flexibility comes into play. It can be fashioned in a wide range of styles: by aging it in oak; on its lees (dead yeast cells spent during fermentation); or entirely in stainless steel to preserve and focus its fruit flavours; or a combination of these and other processes to add layers of flavours to the final wine. Winemaking style greatly affects the flavour, texture, and weight of the finished wine. Not all Chardonnays, then, are created equally, which makes labeling terminology all the more crucial to understand.

If you're a fan of crisp and fruity Chardonnays, you're looking to land an unoaked model. The lack of consensus on labeling however means you'll be staring down everything from non-oaked, unoaked, or no oak designations. Surely, oak free isn't far off.

Also on the lighter side, sur lie Chardonnays are improved with a lush, creamy texture from the winemaking technique of aging the wine on top of its lees. The dead yeast cells impart a pleasant yeasty and nutty flavour to the wine.

Chardonnays that have seen some oak are generally easier to spot; "barrel aged" or "barrel fermented" will be featured prominently on the label, partially to justify the sticker price. Oak aging, particularly when done in French barriques adds to the expense of the finished wine. Oak aging mellows the acidity and fruit and adds hints of toasty vanilla and butterscotch to the finished product. But if not properly handled, it can overwhelm the positive characteristics and make for a clumsy wine.

Think of it like adding spice in cooking. A little taste can perk up a dish, adding depth of flavour and some interest to your meal. Too much can spoil the dish.

The real can of worms in terms of Chardonnay labels is reserve bottles, which are often — but not always — more focused and refined than their barrel-aged brethren. As with other domestic wines, the term 'reserve' is not defined by law. It means essentially whatever the winery wants it to mean. Consumers assume that reserve connotes the vintner's best selection, however the rule is not written in stone.

Tasting Panel: DB, LB, TP, RP, GP, TS, WS, CW

VINES AWARD

Thirty Bench Wines 2000 Benchmark Chardonnay Reif Vineyard Estate

Niagara Peninsula $25

Winemaker Yorgos Papageorgiou is a consistent source for some of Niagara's most distinctive and unique Chardonnays. Working with limited yield fruit from a prime section of Reif Estate Winery's vineyard, he has created a whopper of a Chardonnay that invites comparisons with the best Chardonnays from any wine region you care to mention. This is a concentrated wine with rich viscosity, mineral-like acidity and great length. It is an excellent value for the price and will reward those patient enough to let it age in their cellars. Drink now to 2007.

HIGHLY RECOMMENDED

Burrowing Owl Vineyards 2002 Chardonnay

Okanagan Valley $23 (510933)

It's the little things about this wine that really charm — the subtle floral notes that linger behind the ripe apple and peach fruit aromas, and the creamy lime character that lingers on the finish. Another extremely well-made Chardonnay from a blue-chip producer, Burrowing Owl's 2002 strikes the right chord between heavyweight character and elegant presentation. If you were to personify this wine, the leading contender would be Ali in his prime. Poetic, pretty, but with a force of conviction that'll knock you sideways.

Cave Spring Cellars 2000 Chardonnay CSV

Niagara Peninsula $30 (529941)

The allure of this wine was obvious to all tasters who were bowled over by its deep flavours, richness, and expressive profile. There's a depth of flavour and concentration to this wine that's impossible to miss. There's also an elegance to the presentation that makes this supremely finer than

the blockbuster oak bombs that turned so many consumers off of Chardonnay in the past decade. It will be better given three or more years of aging for the flavours to further integrate and harmonize.

Henry of Pelham Family Estate Winery 2002 Chardonnay Reserve

Niagara Peninsula $13.95 (252833)
Nice, soft, and round Chardonnay that puts its emphasis square on the bright citrus, apple, and pear fruit flavours. A small amount of barrel aging adds to the structure and helps to focus the fruit flavours and adds some complexity to the finish. A great answer for those looking for an affordable white wine for the holiday turkey.

Hillebrand Estates Winery 2000 Chardonnay Unfiltered (Wine Bottled with its Lees)

Niagara Peninsula $35 (981043)
The second vintage of winemaker J-L Groux's special reserve Chardonnay once again proves the method to the madness of bottling an unfiltered Chardonnay. The wine is bottled with its lees (the spent yeast cells from fermentation), which makes the transparent wine bottle look something like a souvenir Snow Globe. The texture is remarkably creamy, thanks, in part, to the wine's extended lees contact. The ripe pear and apple fruit aromas morph into tropical fruit and coconut flavours on the palate. It's a cloudy, but decidedly delicious take on Chardonnay.

Inniskillin Wines 2000 Chardonnay Founders' Reserve

Niagara Peninsula $29.95 (586370)
Inniskillin's Founders' Reserve is establishing a solid reputation as one of Niagara's finest and most consistent expressions of Chardonnay. Ripe fruit and toast aromas and a soft, spicy mouth feel are the hallmarks of the stunning 2000 model. There's a pleasant creamy middle and end to this wine,

and a spicy apple note that gains richness, depth, and nuance on the finish. Drink now to 2009.

Jackson-Triggs Niagara Estate 2001 Chardonnay Delaine Vineyard

Niagara Peninsula $16.95 (623454)

The debut vintage from Vincor chief executive Don Triggs and wife Elaine's expansive vineyard located along the Niagara River, this is a complex and elegant Chardonnay that ranks as one of the finest of Ontario's 2001 vintage. It opens with lush notes of apple and citrus and gains intrigue from vanilla and mineral notes. The bright acidity enhances the tropical fruit and oak flavours. This focused, polished Chardonnay is an ideal dinner companion. Enjoy with grilled seafood or fish.

Jackson-Triggs Niagara Estate 2001 Chardonnay Proprietors' Grand Reserve

Niagara Peninsula $16.95 (593996)

This offers a wonderful expression of Chardonnay, with nicely-integrated oak aromas and flavours. This luxurious, yet affordable wine is precisely the type of Chardonnay in which Niagara has a tremendous advantage over most of the New World wine regions. It's rich, creamy, and extremely well-crafted. It should go well with most chicken, ham, and salmon dishes.

Lailey Vineyard 2002 Chardonnay Canadian Oak

Niagara Peninsula $29

Fennel and anise aromas from the oak merge with attractive caramel toffee and coconut aromas on the nose. That coconut and herbal/spice essence carries over onto the palate, which is buffered by green apple and pear fruit flavours. The wine is round and soft on the palate, and finishes dry with a lingering herbal note. A great partner for dishes with cream sauces or soft cheeses.

Mission Hill Family Estate 2001 Chardonnay Bin 99
Okanagan Valley $14.95 (518530)
Mission Hill produces a range of nicely styled and structured Chardonnays that deliver pleasures that range from simple to sublime. The 2001 Bin 99 hits the mark and offers unbeatable quality for its price. The pure fruit flavour is the main thrill here, which is not to suggest this Chardonnay lacks freshness and elegance. It's well integrated and beautifully crafted.

Peninsula Ridge Estates Winery 2002 Chardonnay Reserve
Niagara Peninsula $39.95
Here's a celestial Chardonnay modeled after the Yin-Yang symbol. There's the full-bore expression of barrel-fermented fruit cut by the laser-like minerality of some of Peninsula Ridge's unoaked Inox Chardonnay. The addition adds a nice counterpoint to massive tropical fruit character and creamy texture. Still a baby, this wine needs time to further integrate and mellow into a rich complex Chardonnay.

Tinhorn Creek Estate Winery 2002 Chardonnay
Okanagan Valley $14.95 (5301691)
Delicate ripe pear and yeasty/bready aromas dominate the nose of this well-made, inexpensive Chardonnay. The panelists commented that the wine's vibrancy offered a nice counterpoint to the creamy mouth feel. Fresh citrus flavours refresh the palate. The price suggests buying in quantity to enjoy over the next two to three years.

Quails' Gate Estate Winery 2001 Chardonnay Family Reserve

Okanagan Valley $29.99 (639641)

Quails' Gate's stellar Family Reserve stands out as a world-class expression of cool-climate Chardonnay. A lightly oaked reserve that puts the focus squarely on the wine's obvious and attractive fruit flavours, this offers bright lemon and citrus fruit with a pleasantly spicy finish. The oak plays a secondary role here, adding a depth of flavour to the palate before fading into the background. Match with seafood or cream pastas for a pleasurable dinner treat.

Township 7 Vineyards and Winery 2002 Chardonnay

Okanagan Valley $16.90

A new winery started by Corey and Gwen Coleman who cut their wine teeth in the Okanagan at a variety of wineries. This small batch Chardonnay comes across as a monster, but it's a softy on the inside. Opens with wafts of banana, pineapple, vanilla and a touch of toast. With some aging on its lees, it has an attractive creamy texture with a core of rich acidity that lifts the tropical fruit flavours. Finishes with a spicy kick. A great start for the Coleman's, and for fans of well-crafted Chardonnay.

RECOMMENDED

Calona Vineyards 2002 Chardonnay Artist Series Reserve

Okanagan Valley $12.99 (559773)

A well-made and affordable Chardonnay that offers interesting popcorn, smoke, and citrus peel aromas. The palate features fresh citrus and melon flavours, with a flinty mineral edge. Great value and widely available in Western Canada.

Cave Spring Cellars 2000 Chardonnay Reserve

Niagara Peninsula $19.95 (256552)

A complex and rich wine, with nice smoke and clove aromas. On the palate, the abundant earthiness and spice character are nicely matched with soft fruit flavours. The aromas are funky and reductive, which kept this from scoring higher for some panelists.

Harbour Estates Winery 2002 Chardonnay

Niagara Peninsula $12.95

When you have big fruit to work with, sometimes a bit stick is required to soften the wine. In this one, there's a lot of typical tropical fruit on the nose with a fine spread of buttery toast notes. On the palate, the oak softens the acids without really interfering with the pineapple, lemon and apple flavours. Although it has a slight tart finish, it's designed to be enjoyed with food.

Hillebrand Estates Winery 2001 Trius Chardonnay Niagara-on-the-Lake

Niagara Peninsula $16.95 (497248)

Crafted with grapes from vineyards located in Niagara-on-the-Lake, this features notes of honeysuckle with butter, vanilla and pear. Really, it's a cross between an elegant Chablis and monster California Chardonnay. It has a core of acidity that enhances the crisp tropical fruit, but there's a lot oak fighting to fit in. Needs time to mesh, or decant before serving.

Hillebrand Estates Winery 1998 Trius Chardonnay Beamsville Bench

Niagara Peninsula $16.95 (291468)

Here's an inexpensive way to taste how Niagara Chardonnay develops with some bottle aging. A regional blend of fruit from the Beamsville Bench that has been barrel-fermented and aged in small oak barrels, this wine exhibits nice apple and butterscotch flavors with some spice and flinty mineral notes. Drink now to 2005.

Inniskillin Wines Okanagan 2001 Chardonnay Dark Horse Vineyard

Okanagan Valley $15.95 (632109)

Picture perfect Okanagan Chardonnay with lots of ripe peach and apple aromas. The delicious fruit is dressed up with some vanilla and butterscotch notes from oak-aging. Inniskillin's single vineyard Chardonnay is round and extremely approachable. Drink now.

Konzelmann Estate Winery 2000 Chardonnay Grand Reserve

Niagara Peninsula $45 (610022)

Konzelmann's Grand Reserve Chardonnay is a whopper of a wine that carries with it a whopper of a price. This is Chardonnay that follows after an Australian model: rich, ripe with creamy peach/nectarine fruit and a seductive palate, thanks to the wine's toasted oak notes and honey-like viscosity. It's a superb wine that's worth the spurge. Try with grilled or cold lobster dishes.

Lailey Vineyard 2001 Chardonnay Old Vines

Niagara Peninsula $39

A monster of wine from David and Donna Lailey's immaculate vineyard on the Niagara River Parkway in Niagara-on-the-Lake, which was initially planted in 1970. True to winemaker Derek Barnett's style, this is big and concentrated with honey, citrus, and spice notes. The wine's obvious heft is nicely balanced by some tart acidity, which makes this mouth-filling Chardonnay opulent as opposed to overblown.

Lakeview Cellars 2000 Reserve Chardonnay Vinc Vineyard

Niagara Peninsula $35 (602557)

Lakeview's single-vineyard Chardonnay serves up a tight, flinty beam of fruit, with citrus and mineral aromas and attractive ripe fruit notes. Nice balance and finish. There's a certain finesse here. Fans of complex flavours and higher acidity will take a shine to this special wine that was barrel fermented and aged for 18 months in French oak. Drink now to 2006.

Magnotta Winery 2001 Merritt Road Vineyard Chardonnay

Niagara Peninsula $8.95

This inexpensive Chardonnay makes a solid first impression with lush notes of pineapple, almonds, and fresh sliced pear. It continues to impress on the palate, with its nice silky, smooth texture and tropical fruit flavours. An elegant Chardonnay, and clearly one of the best from Niagara's 2001 crop.

Mission Hill Family Estate 2002 Chardonnay Reserve

Okanagan Valley $17.95 (545004)

Mission Hill winemaker John Simes is a diligent vintner who has dedicated himself to creating the best wine possible in the Okanagan Valley, and has succeed in shifting the benchmark with each completed vintage. This elegant expression of Chardonnay offers vibrant citrus fruit flavours that are perfumed by delicate floral notes. With lovely texture, this is a great wine to enjoy by the glass or with a wide array of entrées.

Niagara College Teaching Winery 2002 Barrel Fermented Chardonnay

Niagara Peninsula $24.95

Extremely ripe fruit is focused and enhanced by fermentation and 10 months aging in American oak barrels. Tropical fruit flavours and buttery oak essence dominate the wine's creamy palate. A crisp wave of acidity refreshes the flavours on the lingering finish. This beautifully balanced wine will benefit from two to four years of bottle aging.

Nk'Mip Cellars 2000 Chardonnay
Okanagan Valley $15.95 (626408)
The debut Chardonnay from Nk'Mip Cellars (pronounced inkameep), North America's first aboriginal owned and operated winery, offers textbook aromas and flavours. Citrus and vanilla scents perk up the aromatics, while apple and pear notes dominate the wine's creamy texture. In many ways this is a standard issue Okanagan Chardonnay, but rendered with more vibrancy and finesse than is common for wines in this price range. A basic beauty at a great price, it should go well with most chicken and seafood dishes. Drink now.

Peller Estates 2001 Private Reserve Chardonnay
Niagara Peninsula $18.95 (618298)
A shining star from 2001 in Ontario. Expressive citrus and melon characteristics with a touch of buttery oak carry over to the palate. Features blended layers of acidity and oak that keep the wine from getting to soft. Verging on elegant, the restraint with oak keeps this wine in check. A great food wine.

Reif Estate Winery 2002 Premium Select Chardonnay
Niagara Peninsula $10.95 (127977)
Harvested from select vines on the Reif estate, this delightful Chardonnay is a lush, mouth-watering wine. Aromas of pear, green apple and star fruit carry over to the palate. A medium-bodied white, it also features a creamy texture marked by a hint of sweetness. This is a fine wine at a great price.

Strewn Winery 1999 Terroir Chardonnay Strewn Vineyard

Niagara Peninsula $18.95 (542415)

The nose is a mélange of spiced apple and pear notes that carry over on to the rich and creamy palate. Apple and pear fruit marry assertive oak flavours on this well-integrated and slightly warm Chardonnay. It's a wine with good weight and complexity. Enjoyable now for its delicious fruit, it will blossom beautifully in the cellar over the next three years.

Thirteenth Street Wine Co. 2001 Sandstone Chardonnay Reserve

Niagara Peninsula $25

Niagara's boutique winery, Sandstone shifted its style to a more New World expression of Chardonnay, likely in response to the hot 2001 vintage. The flavours are more pure fruit (especially tropical fruit and peach nectar) than funky Burgundy notes from oak aging and winemaking tricks of the trade. Full-bodied and concentrated, this is a powerful reserve.

Thomas and Vaughan Vintners 2000 Chardonnay Estate Reserve

Niagara Peninsula $20

A very attractive Chardonnay that would appeal to those with a penchant for oak. Opens with dense notes of vanilla, pear, and buttery toast. It also features layers of acidity and oak that are softened by malo-lactic fermentation, which gives the wine a creamy, rich body. Coupled with a spicy finish, this is one groovy wine. .

Quails' Gate Estate Winery 2001 Chardonnay Limited Release
Okanagan Valley $15.95 (377770)

There's a line in a Springsteen song, where he tells Rosalita he's not here for business, he's strictly on the scene for fun. Sip this wine and you're bound to be singing the same song. Clean citrus and pear notes, soft acidity and a touch of oak spice make for a Chardonnay that's built for celebrating. Break out the new Essential Springsteen collection, uncork this cool Chardonnay, and get the party started.

Vineland Estates Winery 2000 Chardonnay Reserve
Niagara Peninsula $48

Lighter and more delicate than one might expect from a Reserve Chardonnay, Vineland's 2000 scores points where it counts – drinking pleasure. A fruit-forward wine, boasting plenty of lush tropical and pear fruit packed onto its lithe frame, this is a solid sipping wine and an excellent dinner companion. Serve with grilled veal chops, pork tenderloin medallions, game birds, or pan-roasted sea bass or salmon. Be sure to have another bottle on hand. You'll need it.

QUITE GOOD

Ancient Coast 2001 Chardonnay
Niagara Peninsula $8.75 (559187)

An entry level VQA brand from the Vincor stable, this wine's purpose is to be affordable enough get people to start trying VQA in the under-10 price point. This one opens with a flinty note with green apple and pear lurching in beyond. On the palate, the flinty character lingers, but the fruit is more prominent. It has a touch of oak, but not enough to call it woody. A good buy at the price point.

Caroline Cellars 2001 Chardonnay
Niagara Peninsula $10.95
This newbie winery in Niagara has over four generations of grape growing behind it. Owned by Lakeit Farms, the Lakeit family has joined the ranks of grape producers turned wine producers in the area. Its 2001 Chardonnay opens with attractive notes of banana and pineapple. The acidity explodes on the palate, leaving behind fragments of tropical fruit. Needs to mellow in the glass to round out the acids.

CedarCreek Estate Winery 2001 Chardonnay Estate Select
Okanagan Valley $20 (607200)

A model of crisp and clean Okanagan Valley Chardonnay, with ripe peach fruit, leesy nuttiness and some burnt popcorn notes on the finish. Great with fresh water fish or mild, semi-soft cheeses.

Featherstone Estate Winery 2001 Barrel-Fermented Chardonnay
Niagara Peninsula $16.95
A new kid on the block in Niagara, Featherstone has developed a following based on its commitment to producing estate-grown, insecticide-free wines. This Chardonnay has an interesting note of lemon vanilla custard. One the palate, a deft hand with the oak gives the wine a textured dimension that captures the tropical fruit flavours. Good acidity with a nutty finish caps a well-made wine.

Gehringer Brothers 2002 Dry Rock Chardonnay
Okanagan Valley $12.95 (536169)
Expressive lemon flavours add some excitement to the melon and ripe apple flavour profile. The flavours are focused and the finish lingers, with the slightest kiss of oak spice. Drink now and savour its fresh character.

Hillebrand Estates 2002 Harvest Chardonnay
Niagara Peninsula $10.95 (088385)
A classic cool climate Chardonnay that highlights lemon, pineapple and melon characters with a trace of oak. With its crisp acidity, this a palate cleanser that ends on a tart note. Try this one with a spicy soup or appetizer.

Hillebrand Estates Winery 2001 Trius Chardonnay Lakeshore
Niagara Peninsula $16.95 (291484)
A little lighter than would be expected from a Trius. Features peach blossom, pear and melon with a slight oily texture on the finish. Drink now with lighter dishes or on its own.

Hillebrand Estates 2001 Collectors' Choice Chardonnay
Niagara Peninsula $15.95 (291682)
This Collectors' Choice features a reprint of White Pine by Group of Seven artist A.J. Casson. Lemon dominates from start to fine. Crisp, bright, and clean, this is a tasty Chardonnay for any occasion. A glimpse of buttery oak rounds out the finish.

Malivoire Wine Co. 2002 Chardonnay Estate Bottled
Niagara Peninsula $22 (573147)
A nice expression of the quality of the 2002 harvest, this wine will win you over with its fresh fruit aroma. On the palate, it's focused with an intriguing earthiness and crisp acidity. Its taste is fine and fresh, which makes it a wonderfully versatile wine.

Mission Hill Family Estate 2001 Chardonnay Reserve

Okanagan Valley $17.95 (545004)

Mission Hill's 2001 Chardonnay Reserve is a round and elegant wine with lots of appealing citrus/fruit cocktail and mineral flavours, and long, creamy finish. It's that delicate texture that makes this a standout.

Mountain Road Wine Company 2000 Barrel-Aged Chardonnay

Niagara Peninsula $15.95

Another newbie on the Niagara wine scene, former grape grower Steve Kocsis has switched titles to wine producer. His first vintage is modeled after a Burgundian-styled Chardonnay that places more emphasis on the fruit than on the oak. Opens with notes of pineapple, pears with a hint of flinty mineral. On the palate, there's enough acidity to balance the oak. Nice flavours of pineapple and green apple with soft layers of toasted oak. A thin layer of mineral gives the wine added complexity. Ends crisply.

Pelee Island Winery 2002 Premium Select Chardonnay
Pelee Island $10.95 (21604)

Created from grapes that have been specially selected by the resident viticulturalist, this "premium select" Chardonnay is a refined wine that wins you over with its steely character. With subtle notes of pineapple and peach, the wine doesn't really show its stuff until in the mouth. The finely balanced acidity with soft tones of oak creates a crisp, fresh white with just enough depth to hit the finish line. A little light on the fruit, but with the right food selection, this wine could shine.

Peller Estates 2001 Heritage Series Chardonnay

British Columbia $9.49 (582825)

A great value priced Chardonnay that allows the fruit to take centre stage. Notes include pear and lemon – both of which carry over to the palate. A racy acidity overpowers the oak but makes for a clean, crisp wine. Built for everyday life, this a wine to have chilled in the fridge to enjoy while making dinner.

Reif Estate Winery 1999 Chardonnay Reserve Estate

Niagara Peninsula $19.95 (252163)

Complex aromas of butter, cedar, cream, and subtle melon make for a great first impression. On the palate, the wine scores more points with its up-front fruit and zingy acidity. It's a wine that's all set to go, but the oak is still looming over the fruit so let it decant for a bit.

Sandhill 2002 Chardonnay Burrowing Owl Vineyard

Okanagan Valley $15.99 (541193)

This dry and flinty model of Chardonnay split the panel. Some praised its slightly oily palate that is marked with creamy butter, honey, and vanilla notes. Others offered more muted applause, saying the wine's garlicky and nutty notes make it more interesting than enjoyable.

Summerhill Pyramid Winery 2000 Chardonnay Alchemy

British Columbia $29.95

For people looking to try something different, Summerhill's Alchemy Chardonnay is a magical elixir. Although labeled as a Chardonnay, winemaker Bruce Ewert has added trace amounts of Icewine to give the wine a decidedly different character. Opens with notes of almond, honey, pear and even a dash of mint. The soft fruit carries over to the palate with a viscous mouth feel that provides a little depth. Verging on dry, the Icewine may have been used to soften the acids, which are still in full effect. The wine ends on a tart note. Enjoy with a reading of your future by the local fortune teller.

Stonechurch Vineyards 2001 St. David's Bench Reserve Chardonnay
Niagara Peninsula $22 (569426)
A simple wine that showcases the fresh fruit flavours of Chardonnay. Although this reserve spent time in the barrel, it didn't overpower the fruit. Opens with notes of pear and peach with an every-so-subtle toasty oak. On the palate, the wine's racy acidity creates a crisp, fruity delight. A touch of nut on the finish takes away from some of the fruit, but it's still a fine wine for any occasion.

Stoney Ridge Estate Winery 2002 Bench Chardonnay
Niagara Peninsula $11.95 (292839)
There's always a neat peaches-and-cream element to Stoney Ridge's affordable Bench Chardonnay. Luscious fruit and well-tempered oak tease your tastebuds. Drink now to make the most of its fresh and fruity character.

Thornhaven Estates 2001 Chardonnay
Okanagan Valley $15.90 (724872)
A soft and creamy expression of Chardonnay, with good flavours and a short finish. The wine is a bit one dimensional, but will please a wide variety of palates. Drink now.

Trillium Hill Estate Winery 2000 Chardonnay

Niagara Peninsula $14.95

This is a Gewürztraminer in a Chardonnay bottle. Opens with notes of ginger spice, apricot and peaches. On the palate, more spicy characters with some ripe fruit flavours. Slightly tart on the finish. An interesting take on Chardonnay.

Willow Heights Estate Winery 2001 Stefanik Vineyard Chardonnay

Niagara Peninsula $19.95 (487025)

This single vineyard Chardonnay gets full marks for its lush fruit flavours and its finely handled oak aging. Opens with attractive notes of pear, vanilla and hints of peach. On the palate the wine's acidity come on a bit strong, but the oak tempers it by the finish. Nice flavours of toast, vanilla and some tropical fruit. Would be a fine partner with seafood dishes or with even pork roast.

Unoaked Chardonnay/ Chardonnay Musque

HIGHLY RECOMMENDED

Cave Spring Cellars 2002 Chardonnay Musque

Niagara Peninsula $14.95 (246579)

The best Cave Spring Chardonnay Musque since its sterling 1997 vintage first announced the power and potential of this distinct clone of the popular grape variety. Big fruit flavours turn slightly spicy (lemon grass) and oily as the wine warms up. This is a fabulous selection to partner with holiday turkey and grilled ham garnished with pineapple.

Daniel Lenko Estate Winery 2002 Chardonnay Unoaked

Niagara Peninsula $12.95

Forget everything you've heard about the Chardonnay backlash. This is a delicious wine that makes the most of its fresh fruit flavours. Fresh peach, pear and tropical fruit flavours and aromas abound in this wine that is beautifully balanced and eminently gluggable by the glass.

Gray Monk Estate Winery 2001 Chardonnay Unwooded

Okanagan Valley $14.99 (501114)

A simple and enjoyable Chardonnay that makes the most of its lemon/citrus character. Good acidity and a crisp, long finish make for a most refreshing sipping wine. Those attributes would also match nicely with sautéed scallops on pasta, mussels, or oysters.

Stoney Ridge Estate Winery 2000 Charlotte's Chardonnay Founder's Signature Collection Unoaked

Niagara Peninsula $24.95

Jim Warren's tropical fruit-washed Chardonnay is as much of a mouthful as his wine's wordy title. The debut release from Stoney Ridge's newly-created Founder's Signature Collection sets an impressive tone for the limited edition series. True to Warren's established winemaking style, this wine comes right at you with generous fruit, especially peach, apricot, and pineapple flavours. It's a lush sipping wine tailor-made for the patio or deck.

Thirteenth Street Wine Co. 2002 Sandstone Chardonnay Musque Estate

Niagara Peninsula $18

A beautifully lush and luxe wine that displays the honeyed and floral notes of Alsatian aromatic white as opposed to the toasted oak character common to Chardonnay. The ultra-ripe fruit translated to 14-plus per cent alcohol, which plumps up the palate and leaves fruit sweetness on the finish. Have some fun. Serve this to people who claim they don't like Chardonnay and smile when they ask for the name of the great wine they are drinking.

Quails' Gate Estate Winery 2002 Allison Ranch Un-Oaked Chardonnay

Okanagan Valley $11 (568931)

Deliciously fruity Chardonnay from Quails' Gate's budget friendly Allison Ranch label. Very clean, this is a bright mouthful of wine with a round finish. Perfect as an apéritif or with a light meal.

RECOMMENDED

Henry of Pelham Family Estate 2002 Non-Oaked Chardonnay

Niagara Peninsula $11.95 (291211)

Is that nutmeg? There's a warm spice essence lingering between the wall of citrus and apple fruit aromas and flavours. The panel ultimately couldn't decide which spice note they were searching for. We leave it to you, dear reader, to judge. Email wsendzik1@cogeco.ca and let us know what you think. Good Chard, by the way. Great price.

Legends Estates Winery 2002 Chardonnay Musque

Niagara Peninsula $12.45

This new Niagara producer has a winning way with aromatic white wines, including this fresh and softly perfumed Musque. This expressive wine has developed notes of floral and citrus, and features a medley of fruit flavours, including a touch of exotic fruit. Try it with a goat's cheese salad with mixed greens, red and yellow peppers, and mango or papaya.

Malivoire Wine Company 2002 Chardonnay Musque Spritz

Niagara Peninsula $17

Here's a different approach to Chardonnay Musque, a somewhat whimsical wine that celebrates the Muscat-like aromas and flavours of this special Chardonnay clone. This fresh, fragrant, blossomy beauty has been bottled with a gentle fizziness (hence the Spritz in the name), which adds some interest and excitement on the palate. The effervescence seems to continually refresh the tropical and citrus fruit flavours in this slightly off-dry wine. Extremely easy to drink, with a lower alcohol content (nine per cent), this is a fabulous any place, any time sipping wine.

Mountain Road Wine Company 2000 Chardonnay Unoaked Steve Kocsis Hillside

Niagara Peninsula $14.95

Debut vintage from a new Niagara winery, this unoaked Chardonnay presents apple and pear fruit with some crisp citrus flavours. The palate is concentrated and offers a slight nutty complexity.

Peninsula Ridge Estates Winery 2002 Inox Chardonnay

Niagara Peninsula $29.95 (594226)

This is a lively and appealing unoaked Chardonnay that represents the direction that Peninsula Ridge's French winemaker Jean-Pierre Colas wants to push Canadian Chardonnay. Toasted almond and matchstick aromas add some intrigue to the wine's pleasing fruit character. Full-focused flavours, round texture and a persistent finish are the hallmarks of a considerable, complete wine. Best after 2004.

Vineland Estates Winery 2002 Chardonnay Musque

Niagara Peninsula $18.95

This delicate wine exudes aromas of citrus zest, white flowers, sweet lime and nectarine. The fruit carries onto the palate, which also features a slight mineral overtone. An easy-drinking, versatile wine that can be served by itself or with light-to-medium flavoured meals.

QUITE GOOD

Château des Charmes 2000 Silver Label Chardonnay

Niagara Peninsula $9.95 (636860)

A new release to commemorate Château des Charmes 25th anniversary, the Silver Label Chardonnay adds an affordable unoaked Chardonnay to the Niagara winery's impressive portfolio. The panel liked the peach and yeasty/nutty aromas, and the full, rich flavours on the palate.

Harrow Estates 2002 Chardonnay

Lake Erie North Shore $8.95 (432062)

If you're looking for a refreshing non-oaked Chardonnay, this 2002 offering is one to seek out. Opens with notes of freshly sliced lemon and green apple. Full of citrus flavours, the acidity drives the wine through to a refreshing, crisp finish. Although it doesn't have a "typical" Chardonnay character, it's still a well-made wine that would be great with grilled fish.

Pillitteri Estates Winery 2002 Chardonnay Unoaked

Niagara Peninsula $10.95 (349282)

This is a subtle and straightforward model of Chardonnay with good acidity and positive fruit character. Simple, yet elegant wine made for sipping while catching up on the day's events with loved ones.

GEWÜRZTRAMINER

Can you say Gewürztraminer? If you can —
and you aren't afraid to ask for it by name in a
restaurant — pat yourself on the back, you're in
the minority. Gewürztraminer (pronounced
Ga-vertz-tra-mee-ner) is a highly aromatic white
wine with an unfriendly consumer name. The
word "Gewurz" means spicy or perfumed in
German, and the related Traminer grape is
believed to have originated in the Italian village of
Tramin. Gewürztraminer has fought an uphill
public relations battle ever since.

British wine writers have been known to say the
wine's powerful come-hither aromatics are
"vulgar." Allegedly it's the cheap scent of "a tart's
boudoir," which, in our humble opinion, casts
more aspersions on the authors' character than
on the wines'.

Around the Vines office, Gewürztraminer is
simply the G-wine. We are tracking the rising

production of this great grape in Canada with keen interest. The more, the merrier, indeed.

Making good Gewürztraminer is a balancing act. Winemakers must wait to pick late in the season in order for the full flavour and aroma to develop, but not so late that the grape's notoriously low acidity has dissipated. Gewürz requires a cooler growing season to reach the higher acidity levels necessary for a well-balanced wine.

Gewürztraminer seems to have found an ideal home in British Columbia and Ontario. With acid levels in check, it becomes the winemaker's task to extract the grape's true potential. A hallmark G-wine will be a deep golden colour and have a very perfumed nose with loads of ripe lychee fruit and soapy, rosewater characteristics. Ripe tropical fruit can also make an appearance. Another notable characteristic is the finished wines tend to be fuller bodied, with a higher alcohol range than most whites thanks to the higher sugar levels in the later harvested grapes.

Jackson-Triggs Niagara Estate winemaker Tom Seaver said that choosing when to harvest Gewürztraminer is the important part of the winemaking equation. "If you pick it right, the rest follows suit," said Seaver, who judges a good Gewürztraminer by purity of fruit and good acidity levels. In a rich style of wine, such as Jackson-Triggs Niagara Estate 2002 Delaine Vineyard Gewürztraminer, he will keep the juice in contact with the grape skins to add extract and complexity to the finished wine.

When looking for a benchmark Gewürztraminer, start in Alsace. The small French region's winemakers have pioneered the varietal and consistently produce stellar Gewurztraminer (the region doesn't use the umlaut ü). Germany, Italy, New Zealand, Australia, Chile, California and the Finger Lakes, New York, also produce Gewürztraminer. In Canada, the potential is definitely there.

FOOD PAIRING SUGGESTIONS Well-made Gewürztraminer has a roundness and oiliness which, combined with the wine's alcohol content, enable it to take on the hottest spices and herbs with ease. It is a classic companion for Thai, Szechuan, Cantonese or Indian dishes. Dry Gewürztraminer would be better suited to pork roasts, stews, and casseroles. For best effect, always chill the wine before serving. It really enhances the flavour profile.

Winemakers in British Columbia and Ontario have hit the target, but not on a consistent basis. The 2002 vintage smiled on the aromatic grape variety, thanks to warm and sunny conditions and a long ripening season. Once consistency has been established, Gewürztraminer seems likely to be one of Canada's calling cards on the world market.

Tasting Panel: RD, KM, WS, CW

VINES AWARD

Jackson-Triggs Niagara Estate 2002 Proprietors' Reserve Gewürztraminer
Niagara Peninsula $10.45 (526269)
Who said you had to spend a lot to get that rich Gewürztraminer character? This is a fabulous easy-going wine with bold varietal character and delicious fruit flavours. The 2002 vintage seems to have blessed Niagara Gewürztraminers with the same bright acidity and ripe fruit that is making Ontario's 2002 Rieslings such show-stoppers. A great wine for year-round entertaining.

St. Hubertus Estate Winery Oak Bay Vineyard 2002 Gewürztraminer
Okanagan Valley $12.99 (597229)
St. Hubertus scores with this aromatic charmer that showcases the floral and lychee aromas common to classic Gewürztraminer. A round and engaging wine, it has soft acidity and a hint of sweetness on the palate. The flavours feature ripe peach and citrus fruit, and a nice mineral note in the background, which make this a versatile option for serving on its own or pairing with spicy Asian food.

HIGHLY RECOMMENDED

Gray Monk Estate Winery 2001 Gewürztraminer

Okanagan Valley $13.99 (321588)

A delicious off-dry style of Gewürztraminer, Gray Monk's 2001 offers powerfully attractive spice (ginger) and lychee aromas that had panelists racing to taste. On the palate, the powerhouse wine continues to delight. There's a lot of weight and a delicious mouth-filling oily texture. Ripe peach, lychee and tropical fruit flavours abound, with a dose of Earl Grey tea and spice on the finish. Fresh and balanced, Gray Monk has crafted a stunningly appealing wine that is flavourful enough to enjoy on its own or with Asian cuisines.

Jackson-Triggs Niagara Estate 2002 Delaine Vineyard Gewürztraminer

Niagara Peninsula $22.95 (989350)

The debut vintage of the Delaine Vineyard Gewürztraminer makes an inspiring first impression. The aromas are at once delicate and powerful — orange blossom and rose petal meet ripe mango and spice. The flavours are full and rich, with a nice balance, lingering spice, and tropical fruit finish. The wine's off-dry character makes it extremely approachable right now. A great food wine, this is a suitable match for spinach and citrus salads, white meat dishes or well-spiced (but not too hot) Asian cuisine.

Malivoire Wine Co. 2002 Moira Vineyard Gewürztraminer

Niagara Peninsula $28

This mouth-filling white wine from Malivoire Wine is consistently one of the best examples of this classic variety produced in Niagara. It's a flowery, fruity, spicy, youthful, brash bombshell — nicely concentrated, long, and exotic. What's

more, there's a wonderful paradox — sweet flavours in a dry wine. It's a great wine, but it would be best to cellar it a few years. Collectors will also want to note this is the end of the line for Moira Vineyard Gewürztraminer. Winter damage has prompted the winery to replant the vineyard with Pinot Noir, another grape varietal thriving on that site.

Thirty Bench Vineyard 2002 Late Harvest Gewürztraminer
Niagara Peninsula $23.95
Don't let the late harvest terminology on the label fool you into thinking this is a sweeter wine. It's only slightly off dry, with an amazingly rich and round character, and a spicy and elegant finish. The wine offers classic lychee and floral aromas and flavours. This big wine has enough stuffing to take on Indonesian and Malaysian dishes. We would like to see this on the wine list of every Chinese restaurant within a 200-km radius of the Beamsville winery.

Thornhaven Estates 2002 Gewürztraminer
Okanagan Valley $12.90 (37317)

Gewurztraminer is turning into one of Thornhaven's strong suits. The relative newcomer to the Okanagan has a winning way of crafting benchmark Alsatian style Gewürztraminers, with enticing floral (rose water), lychee, and white pepper aromatics. Sweet peaches and ginger notes dominate the equally attractive flavour profile. This is a sumptuous wine. Nicely made with bright balancing acidity and the right amount of dramatic G-wine character.

Wild Goose Vineyards 2002 Gewürztraminer
Okanagan Valley $14.95 (414748)
Continuing its first-class reputation for aromatic white wine, Wild Goose's 2002 Gewürztraminer offers peach orchard fruit and rosewater aromas. The slightly sweet palate turns up lychee flavours with an elegant anise and floral note. A very lively wine with a lengthy finish, this is a good food wine. Pair with exotic foods, including fish with ginger salsas or sharp cheeses.

RECOMMENDED

Arrowleaf Cellars 2002 Gewürztraminer
Okanagan Valley $13.90
A crackerjack release from an emerging family winery in the Okanagan Centre, the 2002 greets you with a nicely perfumed nose with card-carrying Gewürztraminer attributes. Upfront lychee and ginger notes set the tone for this tempting aromatic wine that thrives on its fruity and spicy components. It shows lighter acidity, but is still well-made. This is a wine to enjoy over the next two years with Asian roasted meat and poultry dishes.

Cave Spring Cellars 2002 Gewürztraminer
Niagara Peninsula $14.95 (302059)
Most panelists agreed this wine is a future star. Like that backwards kid in Bart Simpson's remedial class ("I'm from Canada and they say, I'm a little slow, eh?"), this is currently dumbed down. The aromas are muted and the fruit flavours are cloaked, but there's a weighty mouth feel to this wine that promises to be stunning when it pops into glorious 3D. Buy now. Drink in 2005 or later.

Domaine de Chaberton Estates 2002 Gewürztraminer

Fraser Valley $13.90 (714261)

Citrus fruit dominates the nose, which also contain hints of honeysuckle and roses in full bloom. The fruit characters turn to the sweet spectrum (juicy apricots, peaches, and ripe pears) on the palate. The wine's generous core of fruit is finely balanced by good acidity. It finishes with a clean sweep that leaves a nice spicy warmth on the palate.

Jackson-Triggs Okanagan Estate 2002 Proprietors' Reserve Gewürztraminer

Okanagan Valley $11.95 (543843)

A nice clean and crisp wine that offers invigorating lemon/lime aromas and sweet orchard fruit flavours, Jackson-Triggs Okanagan has made an exceptionally aromatic white wine. It would have scored even higher had it delivered more Gewürztraminer character. Tasters wondered if this had a bit of an identity issue: is it Riesling or is it Gewürztraminer? The consensus was it's tasty. Enjoy it for what it is.

Marynissen Estates 2002 Gewürztraminer

Niagara Peninsula $11.95

Bring the bowl of the glass to your nose and it's unmistakable. Ah, Gewürztraminer. Marynissen's latest offers good varietal character with subtle lychee, passion fruit, and spice aromas. The texture is plump with nice melon fruit flavours joining the party, but the acidity is lower and the wine is a bit leaner than we would have wished. A good wine to drink now with grilled shrimp, pan seared scallops, and fresh water fish served with a mango chutney.

Quails' Gate Estate Winery 2002 Gewürztraminer Limited Release

Okanagan Valley $14.99 (585745)

Quails' Gate seldom disappoints with its pitch-perfect Gewürztraminers, which offer a mix of intense, in-your-face fruit and delicate floral and spice notes that linger in the background like Peter Falk and the other unseen angels in Wim Wenders Wings of Desire. There's a great dramatic tension between the ripe fruit and the zesty citrus-like acidity that cuts through to the refreshing finish.

Sumac Ridge Estate Winery 2002 Private Reserve Gewürztraminer

Okanagan Valley $13.99 (142893)

Sumac has been unleashing Gewürztraminer to wine enthusiasts since the early '80s. With over 20 years of experience, it's almost a given that Sumac's Gewürztraminer ranks above average year after year. The 2002 vintage is a zesty treat that leans towards the citrus side of the fruit spectrum. Flavours of grapefruit and candied lemon dominate with a rich core of acidity that results in a lip-smacking white wine. Great on its own, or with spicy foods.

QUITE GOOD

Angels Gate Winery 2002 Gewürztraminer

Niagara Peninsula $14.95

It would take a long time to grow tired of the fresh tropical fruit notes emanating out of the glass. All that heady and exotic character is lost in translation, as the wine's flavour profile features more tart fruit flavours and a zesty note that is further enhanced by the wine's crisp character. Best with food.

Calona Vineyards 2002 Artist Series Gewürztraminer
Okanagan Valley $12.99 (237453)
A wine made to be enjoyed while basking in the warmth of the sun. Calona's Artist Series G-wine has a bright character because of its fresh and crisp elements. Sweet fruit aromas, particularly citrus and peach, blend with spicy and floral notes. The finish kicks up a pleasant sweetness. Cottage, ahoy!

Gray Monk Estate Winery 2001 Gewürztraminer (Alsace Clone)
Okanagan Valley $13.99 (321596)
Careful vineyard selection is at work behind Gray Monk's Alsace Clone Gewürztraminer. The crisply dry wine boasts good texture and mouth feel, but lacks flavour. Some floral and lemon notes linger. Needs food.

Hainle Vineyards 2000 Gewürztraminer
Okanagan Valley $26.90 (631804)
This makes the most of its best component: an interesting and exotic peach note that dominates the core of sweet fruit on the palate. A tad one dimensional, but a good sipping wine nonetheless.

Harvest Estate Wines 2002 Gewürztraminer
Niagara Peninsula $11.95 (580035)
Beautiful ripe fruit aromas — tangerine, peaches and apricot — and a nice full texture are the hallmarks of this affordable wine. Lower acidity and a sweet-and-sour character on the palate kept this from scoring even higher with the panel. Drink now.

Hernder Estate Wines 2002 Reserve Gewürztraminer

Niagara Peninsula $16.95 (616524)

It's beautifully aromatic nose conveys bright tangerine and apricot fruit and a decaying rose smell, which is not at all unpleasant. The palate doesn't back up the full-bore aromatics, which is lighter and weaker than one might expect. The wine is nicely balanced with a crisp acidity which makes this a versatile food wine.

Hillebrand Estates 2002 Harvest Gewürztraminer

Niagara Peninsula $10.45 (554378)

Another solid expression of Gewürztraminer from Niagara's 2002 vintage. This affordable white offers typical G-wine aromas: peach, apricot and rosewater, and complex, rich flavours. The flavourful wine is off dry, which makes it a great sipping wine, or a good foil for spicy (as opposed to hot) Thai or Asian cuisine.

Hillebrand Estates 2002 Vineyard Select Gewürztraminer

Niagara Peninsula $10.95 (291740)

Looking for a wine to go with Chet Baker? This would be one to enjoy with the Cool Kat of jazz. A delicious offering that captures the simplicity of a Gewürztraminer. Lots of candied lemon and ripe lychee. A sweet hit upfront with a streak of acidity carries the wine to its mouthwatering finish. Picture this — great jazz, a bright summer day and this wine, you can't go wrong.

Lake Breeze Vineyards 2002 Gewürztraminer

Okanagan Valley $13

Lake Breeze unveils a nicely perfumed and balanced wine with a hint of sweetness on the palate and a subtle spice note. Good acidity and extract make for a flavourful wine made for easy chair or dinner table enjoyment.

**Legends Estates Winery 2002
Gewürztraminer**
Niagara Peninsula $12.95
White wine, particularly aromatic whites like
Gewürztraminer, is a real strength for this
emerging Niagara producer. Aromas of ginger
spice and pineapple make for an appealing nose.
The wine's flavour profile is a little tart, but it has
good structure and nice acidity. Drink with
Szechuan dishes.

Strewn Winery 2002 Gewürztraminer
Niagara Peninsula $13.50 (576017)
This wine's prominent pineapple and apricot
aromas had panelists thinking this was a late
harvest Vidal instead of a bona fide
Gewürztraminer. The peach and muted floral
flavours helped to solve the mystery somewhat. It
might not be a true-to-type Gewürztraminer, but
it is a decent white wine that works with or
without food.

Strewn Winery 2000 Terroir Gewürztraminer
Niagara Peninsula $17.95
Strewn's Terroir series is an impressive premium
tier of wines produced from low-yielding
vineyards that guarantee concentrated and
flavourful vintages. This classically styled
Gewürztraminer is an aromatic charmer with
heady floral, spice, and citrus aromas. The wine is
dry but not the least bit bitter or austere. Its
slightly oily texture gains depth and character as
its mineral nuances emerge. An excellent food
wine, especially with seafood.

PINOT BLANC

Considered a mutant of the Pinot Noir family, Pinot Blanc is so far removed from the grape's family tree it was adopted by the Chardonnay family for years and called Pinot Chardonnay. A fringe varietal that is not widely produced on the world stage, some Canadian wineries have taken a turn at trying to make Pinot Blanc a part of their wine family. Winemakers favour this grape because of its habit of ripening early as well as its vigorous and productive capabilities. Although not overtly aromatic, its frequently high acidity and full body allow many producers to design the wine to be consumed with food.

If you're looking for finely crafted, benchmark Pinot Blanc head west. This year's tasting featured twice as many wines from B.C. It appears that winemakers and grape growers in Ontario have moved away from the grape to concentrate on more popular white varietals.

For those with access to B.C. Pinot Blancs, you're in for a treat. The 2002s are delicious fruit bombs. Clearly the Okanagan Valley is a hot spot for the grape. The tasting demonstrated winemakers have developed a knack for crafting well-balanced, delicious offerings.

"We have always had a great admiration for Pinot Blanc in the Okanagan Valley," explained Roland Kruger, winemaker at Wild Goose Vineyards and consistent producers of tasty Pinot Blancs. "It grows so well in the Okanagan and provides excellent fruit qualities after the wine is fermented. It maintains good acid and ripening qualities in the vineyard. It's another one of those varieties that does not garner a lot of respect form the consumer, just like Riesling!"

From the batch that was tasted, Pinot Blanc has found a home in Canada and should get plenty of respect.

Tasting Panel: LB, RD, RH, WS, CW

VINES AWARD

NK'Mip Cellars 2002 Pinot Blanc

Okanagan Valley $13.95 (626432)

The debut Pinot Blanc from Nk'Mip Cellars (pronounced in-ka-meep), North America's first aboriginal-owned and operated winery, is a textbook Pinot Blanc. Opens with notes of lime, kiwi, and a slice of lemon. The palate is the key to this wine's success. Features crisp, but rounded acids and lots of tropical fruit flavours with an added hint of mint. The acids roll through the wine carrying the flavours from start to finish. If the first vintage is any indication from Nk'Mip, their future looks very bright. With B.C. firmly establishing itself as Pinot Blanc country, this one leads the charge.

FOOD PAIRING SUGGESTIONS Depends on the winemaking style. Unoaked Pinot Blanc can be paired with spicy foods such as Asian cuisine, grilled vegetables and steamed shellfish. Oaked offerings would go well with smoked fish, pork roast and other lean meats.

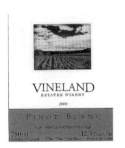

HIGHLY RECOMMENDED

Lake Breeze Vineyards 2002 Pinot Blanc
Okanagan Valley $14

Each year, Lake Breeze manages to produce one of the top Pinot Blanc's in the country. The 2002 offering, which comes from the winery's oldest vines, continues its rich tradition. Aromatics include lemon, grapefruit, and green apple with a touch of spice. The palate features a dose of sweetness which accents the ripe grapefruit and lemon flavours. A core of acidity keeps the wine together without getting in the way.

Vineland Estates Winery 2002 Pinot Blanc
Niagara Peninsula $13.50 (563478)

The marking of a great winery is consistency. Vineland's Pinot Blanc continues to rank as one of the best year after year. The 2002 offering displays fresh fruit flavours of peach and lemon with a core of lively acidity. An added layer of residual sugar is woven into the fabric of the wine giving it an attractive and stylish texture. It's the complete package.

RECOMMENDED

Gray Monk Estate Winery 2002 Pinot Blanc
Okanagan Valley $12.95 (321612)

With its vineyards located in the northern part of the Okanagan Valley and a climate that is suited to the Pinot Blanc grape, this 2002 offering is a fine example of the quality coming out of the Valley. Opens with notes of gooseberry, peach, and lemon. The palate is best described as lush with lots of fruit flavours and a touch of residual sugar that is finely balanced by the acidity. Crisp on the finish, this is one refreshing wine.

Mission Hill Family Estate 2002 Pinot Blanc

Okanagan Valley $13.95 (300301)

No disappointments here. Mission Hill is another winery that consistently produces fine Pinot Blancs. The 2002 vintage opens with classic grapefruit and pineapple notes with an added hint of mint. The palate is a little soft, but there's enough acidity to keep the fruit flavours rolling through to the finish.

Wild Goose Vineyards 2002 Pinot Blanc

Okanagan Valley $12.95 (414722)

Although it comes across like a Gewürztraminer, it gets high marks for its complexity. As intense as a Robert DeNiro stare, it is also chalk full of flavour. Opens with huge notes of peach and pineapple with an appealing floral character. The palate features layers of succulent fruit with an added hint of toast. A little time in oak has rounded the acids creating a wine that would pair nicely with seafood – the standard Pacific Northwest cuisine.

QUITE GOOD

Sandhill 2002 Pinot Blanc

Okanagan Valley $14.99 (541185)

This one is still finding its feet. Having spent some time oak, it's still not fully integrated. Opens with lemon and grapefruit notes with some vanilla undertones. The oak rounds off the acids, but not to the point of muting them. Slightly tart on the finish, a little time in a decanter may just be the tonic to showcase all this wine has to offer.

Strewn Winery 2001 Pinot Blanc

Niagara Peninsula $12.50 (522748)

Another Pinot Blanc that has dipped its toes in oak. Opens with toasty vanilla, lemon and honey notes. Flavours of toast and candied-lemon dominate. A soft white that has enough fruit to make it enjoyable its own.

Sumac Ridge Estate Winery 2001 Pinot Blanc
Okanagan Valley $10.99 (327882)
Although this one has all the markings of a Pinot Blanc, it's a little softer than the others in the tasting. Typical characters of grapefruit and green apple come around on the palate. Lip smacking crisp finish.

PINOT GRIS

In the wine world, Pinot Gris is like the cousin you've always heard the family talk about, but never got the chance to meet. You know, Cousin Larry, a successful something-or-other who lives in a town far away. You get the odd Christmas card from him, but that's about it. In fact, Pinot Gris just happens to be a distant cousin of the popular Pinot Noir grape family, thus the name Pinot Gris, with its greyish blue or brownish pink skin. If Pinot Gris happens to reside in Italy or is made by an Italian-influenced producer, it becomes Pinot Grigio.

In terms of style, Pinot Gris can be made light and spritzy (usually the Pinot Grigio side of the fence) or rich and oily (hello, card-carrying Pinot Gris) depending on the winemaker and vintage. Neither style is overtly aromatic and, when looking for a well-made Pinot Gris, the levels of extraction and acidity are what can make or break the wine. On the international wine scene, critics have picked Pinot Grigio as the next white wine to make a splash with wine consumers. Although Italy and France are leading producers of Pinot Grigio/Gris, Canadian wineries are starting to hit their collective stride with the little grey grape.

In Canada, Pinot Gris is the new kid on the block. With many of the vines under the age of ten, except for some Pinot Gris pioneers in B.C. like Gray Monk, the varietal is too young to have a clear-cut benchmark. Over the past five years, winemakers have moved away from light and airy Pinot Grigio-style wines towards more flavourful and complex wines. Although not as concentrated or adequately honeyed to be compared with Tokay Pinot Gris from Alsace, the winemakers are moving in the right direction.

The Vines Award winner hails from Niagara's Malivoire Wine Company. With nearly ideal conditions for white wine grapes in 2002 in Niagara, the small, boutique winery has released one of the best Pinot Gris on record. "The 2002 vintage was the third harvest for the estate grown Pinot Gris," explained Malivoire winemaker Ann Sperling. "The previous vintages were an opportunity to fine tune the winemaking style and maximize the inherent characteristics of our vineyard. The '02 growing season was short and intense, so our viticultural practice of keeping yields low in the vineyard served to provide fully mature grapes with delicate aromatic fruit, firm acidity and rich flavours with intensity." The result is a truly benchmark wine.

Although the top wine went to a Niagara winery, B.C. wineries are pulling their collective weight with Pinot Gris. Lake Breeze Vineyards winemaker Garron Elmes called the 2002 vintage in the Okanagan Valley "a wine-maker's dream for making fruit-driven wines." According to Elmes, the hot summer and cool fall created ideal conditions for Pinot Gris. "The key to our style of Pinot Gris is acidity as it drives the fruit flavours

FOOD PAIRING SUGGESTIONS
Not too sweet or flowery, Pinot Gris is perfect for fish (both fresh and salt-water), oysters and other shellfish—and any dish with flavours that benefit from the addition of lemon or lime. The acidity and ample fruit of Canadian Pinot Gris make it a match with spicy foods—think Indian, Asian and Middle Eastern cuisine.

and 2002 provide nearly perfect levels of acidity," he explained of his highly recommended wine.

There's a lot of potential for Pinot Gris in Ontario and British Columbia. The submissions demonstrate a commitment by winemakers to develop Pinot Gris to its full potential in Canada.

Tasting Panel: LB, RD, TK, WS, CW, RP

VINES AWARD

Malivoire Wine Co. 2002 Pinot Gris Estate Bottled

Niagara Peninsula $18 (591305)

Winemaker Ann Sperling has done a marvelous job in crafting a truly remarkable wine. Everything came together nicely for Pinot Gris in Niagara in 2002, and Sperling was able to mould the wine into something extraordinary. This high-octane wine opens with exotic aromas of anise, ginger, and peach blossom. The palate displays a small dose of sweetness, followed by a solid nucleus of acidity that lifts the tropical fruit flavours. Higher in alcohol, it's a big Pinot Gris that deserves the top honours.

HIGHLY RECOMMENDED

Kacaba Vineyards 2002 Pinot Gris

Niagara Peninsula $20

Just down the road from Malivoire, Kacaba has managed to kick out a hard core Pinot Gris. Built in the classic style one would find in Alsace, it's a refined wine with lots of character. Opens with notes of white currant, peach, and pineapple with hints allspice. Fruit flavours of apple and lemon dance across the palate. A lively wine with just the right amount of acidity to make it a real treat at the dinner table. Ends on a vivacious, crisp, tart note.

Lake Breeze Vineyards 2002 Pinot Gris
Okanagan Valley $14

An off-dry delight that tantalizes the taste buds. Opens with classic notes of lemon and lime peel. Flavours include peaches and pineapple which are accented by a touch of sweetness up front. Balanced acidity creates a refreshing wine designed for whimsical times on the patio.

Legends Estates Winery 2002 Pinot Gris
Niagara Peninsula $13.50

This start-up winery located on the bench in Niagara is making waves with its 2002 releases. This one is a classic example of a refined Pinot Gris. From its salmon-pink hue through to classic aromas of grapefruit and lemon with a dash of spice, it's a classic. The dominate fruit character is grapefruit and when paired with round acids and a spicy ginger finish, you can only tip your hat to this fine wine.

Mission Hill Family Estate 2002 Pinot Grigio
Okanagan Valley $15.95 (563981)

With winemaker John Simes' accent, there's no mistaking he's not of Italian lineage, but his Pinot Grigio could pass for a southern Italian white. This one features lime and lemon notes with a touch of mint. The flavours are citrus with a solid heart of acidity. The only fingerprint Simes leaves is a slight up front sweetness, something most Italian Pinot Grigios don't have.

Peller Estates Heritage Series 2001 Pinot Gris
Okanagan Valley $12.99 (615559)

A wine that reflects the heritage of the Peller family's great history as pioneers in the Canadian wine industry. This consumer-friendly white manages to hit all the key notes for a Pinot Gris. Opens with lush notes of peach blossom and star fruit. Tropical fruit flavours abound with a band of acidity that manages to keep the off-dry style in check. A dash of toasty oak on the finish enhances its crisp finish. Calls for grilled fish.

Stoney Ridge Estate Winery 2002 Pinot Grigio
Niagara Peninsula $11.95

Although this is not a "typical" Pinot Grigio, it gets high marks for being simply delicious. With exceptional fruit from the 2002 harvest, winemaker Liubomir Popovici, has wired up a fruit bomb. Opens with explosive notes of banana, peach, and freshly sliced pineapple. The tropical fruit shifts to the palate with a hit of sweetness on the front and lots of acidity on the back. Best description – fruit cocktail in a bottle.

RECOMMENDED

Blue Mountain Vineyards 2002 Pinot Gris
Okanagan Valley $19.95

Another high octane burner that puts its alcohol to good use. Although the nose is muted with soft tones of grapefruit, the palate is the focus of this wine. The high alcohol content with the ripe fruit creates an unctuous mouth feel that finishes with a hot flash. A perfect match for spicy foods.

Colio Estate Vineyards 2002 Pinot Grigio
Lake Erie North Shore $13.95 (503391)

Winemaker Carlo Negri has crafted a wine that reaches back to his Italian heritage. With its steely character, it opens with mineral stone and citrus notes. Fruit flavours include grapefruit, lemon, and a layer of mineral. Crisp, clean and refreshing, it ends with a flash of heat. Suited for Mediterranean seafood dishes.

Creekside Estate Winery 2002 Pinot Gris

Niagara Peninsula $15.95

A paint-by-number Pinot Gris that stays within the lines. Driven by a core of acidity, it's a lively wine that focuses mainly on the citrus side of Pinot Gris. Held together by a good dose of acidity, it's lip-smacking crisp with a hot finish.

Gray Monk Estate Winery Odyssey 2001 Pinot Gris

Okanagan Valley $19.99 (620369)

It's not a Space Odyssey, but the journey for this wine started back in 1976 when George and Trudy Heiss decided Pinot Gris was suitable for the northern climate of the Okanagan Valley. A designated reserve, this Odyssey has lovely notes of lanolin, lemon, and lime. Its off-dry style accents the fruit flavours. With its refreshingly crisp finish, it's an ideal wine with which to entertain.

Hawthorne Mountain Vineyards 2001 Pinot Gris

Okanagan Valley $16.99 (704999)

A consistent producer of versatile Pinot Gris, Hawthorne Mountain's 2001 offering has unique characters of peach blossom, anise, and grapefruit. Designed with a touch of sweetness, the acids balance the fruit providing layers of complexity that add to the wine's character.

Magnotta Winery 2002 Special Reserve Pinot Gris

Niagara Peninsula $10.95

If you're looking for a dry white to pair with your favourite catch of the day, give this Pinot Gris a try. Enchanting notes of peach blossom, apricot, and apple highlight the fragrance of the wine. The palate features crisp acidity which highlights the citrus flavours. Ends with a crisp zing.

Pillitteri Estates Winery 2002 Pinot Grigio

Niagara Peninsula (349183)

This tip-of-the-hat to the old country has all the markings of a classic Italian Pinot Grigio.

As one panelist described, "it's got the eye of the partridge colour." Its pinkish hue, typical in southern Italian Pinot Grigio, gives way to orange, lemon, and peach notes. Its dry style highlights more citrus flavours complete with a zesty finish. Best enjoyed with seafood.

Thomas & Vaughan Vintners 2002 Pinot Grigio

Niagara Peninsula $14.95

It's like the remake of the Italian Job. You know the storyline and how it ends, but you still enjoy it. Opens with notes of lemon, peach and, an interesting pine needle scent. Designed as an off dry, there's enough acidity to balance the sweetness. A lively finish rounds out a charming sipper.

Wild Goose Vineyards 2002 Pinot Gris

Okanagan Valley $13.95 (536227)

Keeping in line with the winery's tradition of producing wildly aromatic whites with lots of fruit, this Pinot Gris opens with notes of star fruit, baked apple, and lemon. Although designed to be dry, there's a trace of residual sugar that helps lift the fruit to its crisp finish. A delicious treat for a Sunday afternoon.

QUITE GOOD

Domaine de Chaberton 2001 Pinot Gris

Okanagan Valley $13.95 (627638)

Like a teeter-totter, this one goes back and forth. Opens with lots of tropical fruit notes, but the high acids on the palate counter the fruit flavours. Finishes with a crisp, tart zing. Pair with a salad that features a spicy, tart dressing.

Gray Monk Estate Winery 2001 Pinot Gris
Okanagan Valley $13.99 (118638)
There's lots of character in this wine. Notes of ginger, apricot and lemon open the wine. The palate features grapefruit, lemon, and lime peel. A little soft on the palate, there's enough fruit to tantalize the tastebuds. Crisp, clean finish caps a fine wine.

Inniskillin Wines 2002 Pinot Grigio
Niagara Peninsula $11.95 (348979)
A classic Italian-styled Pinot Grigio, this one opens with a light floral fragrance with some pear and lime notes. Lighter on the acids, the palate displays flavours of green apple, and lemon. A crisp finish crowns this food-friendly wine.

Pelee Island Winery 2002 Pinot Gris
Pelee Island $10.45 (326413)
A soft white that leans on the fruit to make it an appealing consumer-friendly wine. Highlights include grapefruit and lemon flavours with light acids. Built for those who prefer soft over crisp white wines.

Peller Estates 2002 Heritage Series Pinot Gris
Niagara Peninsula $10.50 (615559)
Not as developed as its Okanagan Valley brethren, there's enough fruit and acidity in this Pinot Gris to make it good match for all-you-can eat pan fried perch. Features a zesty, crisp finish.

Summerhill Estate Winery Pyramid Cellar Aged 2001 Pinot Gris
Okanagan Valley $16.95 (714741)
This mystic Pinot Gris has spent some time in the popular pyramid cellars located on the Summerhill property. The aroma profile includes peach and pineapple with a hint of flinty mineral. Designed as an off-dry, it has a sweet lemon character. Lighter acids make for a wine best suited for sipping on the deck.

RIESLING

If you want definitive proof that wine writers have minimal influence on wine trends, look no further than Riesling. Writers of purple-stained prose love it so much, they often become zealous missionaries who try to convert the world to the steely wine that – in its prime – offers orchard-fresh fruit and a live wire of acidity in every glass. Consumers, meanwhile, remain non-plussed.

Year after year, with dogged determination and eternal optimism, the articles arrive with screaming headlines: The Rise of Riesling! Riesling's Revenge! Save Your Soul, Stop Drinking Chardonnay! It makes otherwise civilized and urbane minds sound like the drooling Brother John character in the Bugs Bunny cartoon, Rabbit Hood. "D'uh, don't you worry, never fear, Robin Hood will soon be here…"

Pity poor Riesling. The world's noble white wine grape seems destined to live forever in the shadow of easy-to-drink, easy-to-pronounce, Chardonnay. The pride of Germany, Riesling is an agreeable drink that's all about the balance of fruit and acidity in the finished wine.

Unlike the prima donna Chardonnay, there's no performance-enhancing oak aging, no special additional fermentation to soften the wine or mellow its expressive flavours. Riesling is down-to-earth, a low-maintenance kind of wine. What you see in the grape is what you get in the glass.

Transplanted in any wine region of the world, it will reflect the unique soil and microclimate of the site, yet remains unequivocally Riesling. Its identity is bulletproof. In Canada, it performs exceptionally well, and winemakers are able to consistently produce wines that range from bone-dry to opulent and sweet. We're interested in drier styles here; the sweeter dessert wines are featured later in the book.

A highly aromatic wine, which offers predominantly honey, fruit cocktail and floral notes in British Columbia, or citrus, lime, and floral notes in Ontario vintages, Riesling will develop more of a characteristic kerosene/petrol note as it ages. While Riesling has the capacity to cellar for a long time, most consumers enjoy the young fruit characteristics of the wine as opposed to its aged grease-monkey notes.

For consumers, the upside to Riesling's second-class-citizen status means savvy wine shoppers have their pick of value-priced wines. On a value-for-money axis, it doesn't get any better than undervalued Rieslings, which generally retail in the $8-$12 range. Top producers, looking to create the ultimate expression of Canadian Riesling, are crafting signature reserve wines that are priced $20 and up. The increase in price is attributed to the lower yields harvested in the vineyards.

From his vantage, Brian Schmidt, winemaker at Niagara-based Riesling specialist Vineland Estates, quality Riesling is traced back to its vineyard.

FOOD PAIRING SUGGESTIONS Dry Rieslings are the most versatile white wines on the market for matching with diverse cuisines, such as Thai, vegetarian, French, Mexican and California fusion. It also goes well with appetizers, fried foods, freshwater and saltwater fish, pasta, stir-fries and salads, particularly dishes with citrus flavours. Off-dry styles are excellent sipping or apéritif wines.

Vineland Estates has had a sterling pedigree for Riesling since it was founded by a German winemaker and nurseryman Hermann Weis, the man behind Mosel producer St. Urbans-Hof. After travelling to Washington State and British Columbia, Weis proclaimed the Niagara Bench to be ground zero for the New World Riesling revolution.

"I continually thank Hermann for the foresight," says Schmidt, whose 2002 Dry Riesling earned a five star rating. (It's a back-to-back win. His 2000 Dry Riesling won the Vines Award in our 2003 Buyer's Guide).

Schmidt explains vineyard site and cool fermentation, which help to retain the wine's fruit intensity and flavour, are the keys to crafting world-class Riesling.

Riesling is harder to produce than Chardonnay, which can be crafted and redefined by oak-aging and secondary malo-lactic fermentation. Vineyard sites are crucial for Riesling because the wine is made on the vine. Press the fruit and get out of the way.

The best of these wines can stand shoulder to shoulder with any Riesling exported into this country. This is a variety we can do exceptionally well in Ontario and British Columbia— and, not resting on their laurels, our winemakers continue to ratchet up the quality and finesse of these sublime wines.

Of course, the exceptional growing season afforded both wine regions in 2002 certainly helped the matter. The warm weather made for ideal ripening and great wines across the board — Riesling was especially favoured.

"It's probably our best vintage since 1989," reports Angelo Pavan, winemaker at Cave Spring Cellars in Jordan, Niagara's other Riesling specialist. "I really do mean that, because it ripened and we got the flavours, but there's also beautiful acids. I'm not sure why we had such high acids in a warm year. The aromatic profile is classic. The dry Riesling is really perfumed, really citrusy – it blows away our Sauvignon Blanc. It's that intense."

Tasting Panel: LB, TG, GP, WS, CW

VINES AWARD

Vineland Estates 2002 Dry Riesling

Niagara Peninsula $9.95 (167551)
For the second consecutive year, our panel had the floor yanked out from under them by a zesty, flavourful wine best summed up with one word — electric. Peach and citrus flavours, with a slight flinty mineral note, ride a wave of zesty acidity to a long, long finish. A beautiful wine at a great price, Vineland's dry Riesling offers solid value and straightforward pleasure. It's versatile, useful and ready to drink, though it will gain added complexity with bottle age. Drink or hold. Best from 2004 through 2009.

HIGHLY RECOMMENDED

Cave Spring Cellars 2002 Riesling Dry

Niagara Peninsula $11.95 (233635)
This is an aromatic and extremely aristocratic model of Riesling with zesty citrus notes (particularly lemon and grapefruit) and some slight kerosene notes. Despite its crisp and dry profile, there's a nice depth of flavour that makes this incredibly appealing to drink. The flavours are intense, including some floral and perfume notes along with a hint of honey and kerosene. This will develop nicely over time, but that zingy character is pretty hard to resist right now.

VINELAND
ESTATES WINERY

DRY RIESLING
VQA • NIAGARA PENINSULA • VQA
750 ml   11.0% alc./vol.

CAVE SPRING

Reserve   2002   Réserve
RIESLING
VQA NIAGARA PENINSULA VQA
ESTATE BOTTLED

CAVE SPRING CELLARS, JORDAN, ONTARIO, CANADA
12.0% alc./vol.   750 mL

Quails' Gate Estate Winery 2002 Dry Riesling Limited Release

Okanagan Valley $14.99 (308312)

A thrilling discovery from the Okanagan Valley, this Riesling is absolute magic. "I want to buy it by the case," wrote one smitten panelist. It has pretty much everything — mouth-filling fruit refreshed by racy acidity and a remarkably long, subtle finish of melon and lemon. It's steely character and intense, concentrated flavours (predominantly lime and grapefruit with lingering honey overtones) are bound to impress, particularly when paired with some grilled citrus tuna. Enjoy over the next three to five years.

Vineland Estates 2000 Reserve Riesling

Niagara Peninsula $23 (316307)

This luxurious, yet still reasonably affordable wine sets the mark for Canadian Riesling with bright grapefruit, lime, and intense mineral flavours on the palate. Its rich concentration and balanced acidity suggest a long life for this classic wine that loves food. It can hold its own against highly spiced dishes and exotic flavours too.

Wild Goose Vineyards 2002 Riesling

British Columbia $12.95 (414730)

Wild Goose is a name that fans of aromatic white wine need to know. The Kruger family has a sterling reputation for sweetly perfumed wines that are absolutely killer. They are a consistent source for some B.C.'s finest Rieslings. Our panel loved the honey and peach aromas/flavours of this wine that gain added appeal from some smokey bacon and intense grapefruit notes. An equally arousing palate matches the evocative aromas — it's instant romance.

CSV
Estate Bottled

CAVE SPRING
2002
RIESLING
VQA NIAGARA PENINSULA VQA
CAVE SPRING CELLARS, JORDAN, ONTARIO, CANADA
WHITE WINE/PRODUCT OF CANADA • VIN BLANC/PRODUIT DU CANADA
11.0% alc./vol.   750 mL

RECOMMENDED

Cave Spring Cellars 2002 CSV Riesling
Niagara Peninsula $30 (566026)
If this review were a hockey card, it would be emblazoned as a Future Star. Cave Spring's latest top-tier CSV Riesling is a tad restrained at present, but it has enough depth and concentration to promise a great future. An off dry Riesling built for the long haul, its bright pear/peach fruit aromas and flavours currently mask some delicate leesy and licorice notes which add some intrigue to the wine's enjoyment. Our advice is buy now, drink later. There's no chance this will be available to buy when it is drinking at its peak. Best after 2005.

Cave Spring Cellars 2002 Riesling Off-Dry
Niagara Peninsula $11.95 (234583)
An elegant and extremely appealing wine that offers textbook Riesling character: mineral richness, ripe peach flavours and a very light touch of sweetness which adds fullness to the palate while remaining dry to taste. This is lovely to drink now by the glass, and will partner with most sautéed, broiled, or grilled seafood or pork/poultry dishes.

EastDell Estates 2002 Riesling
Niagara Peninsula $11.95
Enjoyably crisp and appealing model of Riesling produced from fruit sourced from three Beamsville, Ontario vineyards. Floral and ripe fruit aromas, especially white peach and pineapple, standout. On the palate, the wine has an enjoyable weight and some appealing toffee notes peaking out from behind citrus fruit flavours. The wine's hint of residual sugar make it a pleasant sipping wine. Enjoy with a maple-cured or glazed salmon dish.

Gray Monk Estate Winery 2002 Riesling
Okanagan Valley $12.95 (321604)
A number of tasters remarked on this wine's tangy nature. Fresh lime notes invigorate the candied fruit cocktail and apple fruit flavours. Off dry and medium-bodied, this is a wine that loves to party. Serve it with a variety of appetizers, including mussels, scallops, and soft cheeses.

Henry of Pelham Family Estate Winery 2002 Off-Dry Riesling
Niagara Peninsula $14.95 (557165)
That appealing fresh lime character so common in Henry of Pelham's Rieslings is enhanced by just the right touch of mild sweetness and refreshing acidity. The label says off dry; the integrated palate finishes dry. Fresh and youthful, it is lovely now as the perfect everyday food wine. It also has a great future.

Hillebrand Estate 2002 Trius Riesling Dry
Niagara Peninsula $14.95 (303792)
This high-end Riesling has all the elements to warrant the Trius label. Opens with wonderful notes of freshly sliced pineapple with a subtle hint of flint. Fine lines of acidity accentuate the citrus fruits with an every so slight dash of natural sweetness. This will age gracefully — and can be enjoyed now in its youth.

Jackson-Triggs Okanagan Estate 2002 Dry Riesling
Okanagan Valley $10.99 (543835)
It's hard not to appreciate this wine's tropical fruit aromas and flavours, which smell a bit like Carmen Miranda's headdress. It's a charming, easy-to-drink white that is pleasant by the glass, or with a wide assortment of light warm weather fare. It boasts a ripe core of fruit and balanced acidity that suggest this as a great candidate for mid-term cellaring. Drink now to 2008.

Jackson-Triggs Niagara Estate 2001 Delaine Vineyard Riesling

Niagara Peninsula $16.95 (623562)

Delaine is a cute contraction of the names of vineyard owners Don and wife Elaine Triggs, who outfitted their vineyard with the latest clones and rootstocks in an effort to produce the very best fruit. One taste of this pleasing wine is all you'll need to see the logic in all that exacting detail. Richly concentrated with pure citrus and pear fruit that gains complexity from flinty mineral and petrol notes, the Delaine Riesling is neither sweet nor dry. It is extremely tasty by the glass.

Konzelmann Estate Winery 2000 Riesling Grand Reserve Classic

Niagara Peninsula $39.95 (605378)

Konzelmann's Grand Reserve Classic is extremely aromatic and very tasty, but the delicate wine lacks the authority of its exclusive price. On the palate, it is fruity and moderately sweet, with good expression of the varietal, including peach flavours and nice zesty acidity. Floral aromas and mineral green apple flavours make for a wonderful sipping wine.

Pinot Reach Cellars 2002 Old Vines Riesling

Okanagan Valley $14.95 (478461)

A classical style with focussed honeyed apricot and tropical fruit aromas, this showcases Pinot Reach's winning ways with Riesling. The Old Vines on the label signifies that the fruit comes from the first Riesling vines planted in B.C., which date back to May 1978. Best enjoyed with a meal, particularly halibut and grilled vegetables, cheese fondue, or seafood pastas with light cream sauces. Drink now to 2006.

Vineland Estates 2002 Riesling Off-Dry

Niagara Peninsula $9.95 (232033)

The off-dry companion to Vineland's Vines Award winner impressed our panel with its balance of crisp acidity and richly concentrated fruit. Its delicious core of fruit (which includes the usual lemon/citrus range of fruit along with the surprising gooseberry) is cut with a quicksilver seam of acidity that refreshes the flavours on the finish. Dynamite wine to have around for your home entertaining needs.

Wild Goose Vineyards 2002 Riesling Dry Stony Slope

British Columbia $14.95 (434316)

This single-vineyard Riesling delivers candied apricot and honeyed tropical fruit aromas and flavours. Despite the label's claim of being dry, this soft wine is far from bitter or austere. Its lower acidity makes it a natural selection for light-to-medium flavoured meals, including grilled ham and pineapple.

QUITE GOOD

Angels Gate Winery 2002 Süssreserve Riesling

Niagara Peninsula $13.95

A solid expression of Riesling, this off-dry wine is balanced with plenty of attractive fruit and flinty mineral flavours that are the hallmarks of a classic Germanic winemaking style. Finishes clean and dry. Excellent food wine.

Cave Spring Cellars 2002 Riesling Reserve Estate

Niagara Peninsula $15.95 (286377)

There's a delicious core of fruit lurking behind the concentrated earthy, nutty accents. It's a lush wine with nicely evolved flavours and a good depth of flavour with a nervy acidity driving the lingering finish. Best after 2005.

Château des Charmes 2001 Riesling
Niagara Peninsula $9.95 (061499)
A lean model of Riesling that features baked pear and lemon fruit flavours and serious structure. Extremely well-made, this is a bottle built with the dinner table in mind. It will partner with a wide assortment of meals, including Thai food, spicy salads, or steamed fish.

Cilento Wines 2001 Riesling Reserve
Niagara Peninsula $10.95 (605725)
Cilento's signature style is an elegant, slightly austere Riesling, which displays chalky mineral characters and pleasantly peachy /gooseberry overtones. Very refreshing with lots of lemon zest on the finish. It's not for everyone, but fans of crisp, dry wines take note.

Daniel Lenko Estate Winery 2002 Reserve Riesling
Niagara Peninsula $12.95
Here's a model of Reserve Riesling that is fruity and a little bit fun. Like those old CountryTime Lemonade commercials used to boast, it's not too tart, not too sweet. Made in a pleasant, easy-drinking style, this is an excellent wine to serve with all kinds of fish and white meat dishes or for patio sipping in the warmer months.

Featherstone Estate Winery 2002 Riesling Estate
Niagara Peninsula $10.95
Complex aromas, including pretty floral/linden notes and, surprisingly, red licorice are bound to stir up some interest. The palate doesn't quite match — it's mainly peach with a hint of wet stone. A pleasant sipping wine, it's just the thing with which to greet guests as you point them towards a welcoming deck chair.

Harbour Estates Winery 2002 Riesling
Niagara Peninsula $10.95
Riesling has become the stock-in-trade for
Harbour Estates, which consistently produces
classically-styled Niagara Rieslings that are clean,
crisp, and oh so enjoyable when the sun is high in
the sky. Nice lime, lemon and apple fruit marries
with a zesty streak of acidity. Drink now.

Harvest Estate Wines 2002 Dry Riesling
Niagara Peninsula $8.95
Classic aromas and bright citrus flavours on the
palate are hallmark Niagara Riesling. The wine is
lively and beautifully balanced. It's perfect as an
apéritif or with light dishes. Drink now.

Henry of Pelham Family Estate Winery 2002
Dry Riesling
Niagara Peninsula $10.95 (268375)
Aromatic white with typical lime/citrus and grass
aromas, and a nice round mouth-feel. The panel
praised the wine for its balance, mineral and fruit
flavour profile, and lingering finish.

Henry of Pelham Family Estate Winery 2000
Reserve Riesling
Niagara Peninsula $12.95 (283291)
Intense aromas of lime and citrus are featured in
this crisp and lean reserve Riesling. There's a lot of
fresh acidity on the palate, but it's lacking in fruit.
On the whole, harmonious and nicely balanced.
Drink now.

Hernder Estate Winery 2002 Riesling
Niagara Peninsula $9.95 (332239)
Ripe peach aromas and candied fruit flavours
standout in this enjoyable wine, which is built for
anyone looking for a little residual sweetness in
their wine. Best served by the glass or with light
cheeses, or smoked fish appetizers.

Hillebrand Estates 2002 Harvest Riesling
Niagara Peninsula (088377)
An accessible Riesling that features candied
lemon notes. The palate is dominated by citrus
flavours with a dry core. A hint of natural
sweetness hits on the mid-palate. A tart finish
means it needs to be enjoyed with food.

Inniskillin Wines 2002 Late Autumn Riesling
Niagara Peninsula $9.95 (219543)
Distinct aromas of citrus, apple blossom and
honey make for a wonderful first impression, but
unfortunately the palate fails to cash in. Nice
weight and decent intensity, this is a nice wine for
drinking over the next year or two.

Jackson-Triggs Niagara Estate 2002 Riesling Proprietors' Reserve
Niagara Peninsula $9.95 (526277)
Despite the posh Proprietors' Reserve title, this is
an unassuming wine that makes friends easily.
Delicious ripe fruit flavours with good intensity
and balance make for a great any place, any time
sipping wine. As one taster noted, "it's simple, but
pleasurable."

Lakeview Cellars 2002 Riesling
Niagara Peninsula $9.95 (307157)
Balanced acidity and good core of citrus fruit are
the hallmarks of this pleasing dry white wine. The
addition of 15 per cent Kerner increases the
wine's structure and makes it a solid food wine,
especially when tag-teamed with roasted pork or
chicken and fruit chutney.

Legends Estates Winery 2002 Riesling Dry Rosomel Vineyards
Niagara Peninsula $10.75
Approachable, if one-dimensional, Riesling that
makes the most of its intense aromatics: lime,
grapefruit and floral notes. Soft on the palate with
a short finish.

Magnotta Winery 2002 Riesling Medium Dry
Niagara Peninsula $8.85
An ideal summer wine that's built for a lazy weekend — just add a Muskoka chair, the Saturday Globe and Mail and maybe a handful of grapes and some cubed Havarti. There's some persistent lime flavours poking out from the wine's sweet palate. Chill the wine and your mind will follow.

Maleta Vineyards 2000 Reserve Riesling
Niagara Peninsula $15
Since its inception, Maleta has established a house style of Riesling made in the tradition of German Auslese wines. Winemaker/owner Stan Maleta isn't afraid of leaving a substantial amount of residual natural sugar in his wine, even when most consumers gravitate towards drier Rieslings. This is an appealing off-dry wine with lingering lemon flavours and a sweetness on the finish that will delight fans of sweeter whites.

Peller Estates 2002 Riesling Heritage Select
Okanagan Valley $9.95

Easy-drinking wine that delivers tangerine and honey flavours and balanced acidity. It has enough fruit and fat to enjoy on its own, and would make a nice picnic or brunch wine. Drink now.

Peller Estates 2002 Private Reserve Dry Riesling
Niagara Peninsula (981290)
Opens with an attractive floral bouquet that gives way to pineapple and lemon on the palate. With its dry design, it is definitely crisp, but also a tad tart. Needs dishes designed for high acidity wines to be best enjoyed.

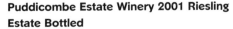

Puddicombe Estate Winery 2001 Riesling Estate Bottled

Niagara Peninsula $TBA

Newcomer Puddicombe Estate is establishing a reputation for itself as a quality producer of aromatic white wines. This is noteworthy for its bright aromas and slightly perfumed finish.

Quails' Gate Estate Winery 2002 Riesling Family Reserve

Okanagan Valley $23 (50005)

A delicious Riesling marked with minerally and steely citrus notes, this wine has lovely concentrated fruit flavours but lacks backbone. Extremely crowd-pleasing style of wine; our panel would have liked to see a bit more structure supporting all of the glorious fruit.

Ridgepoint Wines 2002 Off-Dry Riesling

Niagara Peninsula $9.95

A new cat on the Niagara wine scene, Ridgepoint is located down the road from Lakeview Cellars on Cherry Avenue in Vineland, Ontario. This semi-sweet number opens with notes of freshly squeezed lemon juice. Candied lemon drops best capture the flavour with a crisp layer of acidity that rounds out the sweetness. The finish is a tad tart, but with the right dish — say pan seared Walleye — this would fit right in.

Ridgepoint Wines 2002 Riesling

Niagara Peninsula $9.95

This one leans toward the off-dry scale but manages to keep it dry with a good dose of acidity. Features tart citrus characters throughout the wine. A twist of sweetness adds a touch of complexity. Bait the hook and let this one chill for when the fish bite.

St. Hubertus Estate Winery 2001 Riesling

Okanagan Valley $10.99 (345009)

Classic expression of Okanagan Valley Riesling,
with vibrant floral and delicate honey notes. The
palate turns the spotlight on the wine's intense
lime and Gala apple flavours. Sweet and flavourful
enough to serve on its own, its balanced acidity
makes it a nice match for ginger-flavoured not-
too-spicy Asian dishes or mild curries.

Thirty Bench Wines 1999 Riesling Limited Yield Semi-Sweet

Niagara Peninsula $19.95

Peaches and a honeyed sweetness standout on
the palate of this lush and slightly oily wine.
Drinking well now. Best enjoyed with a selection
of fresh berries and cheeses or medium spiced
Indian curry or Mexican dishes.

Willow Heights Winery 2002 Riesling

Niagara Peninsula $10.95

A lighter, off-dry Riesling with a nice honeyed
peach character that is best consumed in the
coming year. Its low acidity gives it a mellow
mouth-feel. This is best suited as a pre-dinner
sipping wine.

SAUVIGNON BLANC

Wines produced from Sauvignon Blanc offer freshness, flavour and a real concentration of fruit that is best enjoyed young. The classic white's characteristic zestiness is one of its charms. Age dulls that most recognizably Sauvignon Blanc note and, in turn, dulls the enjoyment of the wine. Call this the wine world's equivalent of a one-hit wonder — a glorious burst of fame than nothing but a fleeting residual vapour trail.

Other classic varietal characteristics include: gooseberries; cut grass or other herbaceous notes like asparagus and green peppers; figs; green apples; grapefruit; and cat pee (yes, cat pee; don't wince). Archetypal French Sauvignon Blanc from Sancerre and Pouilly-Fumé can offer a whiff of, how do you say, *pipi de chat*. You might, however, be happy to hear that there's little tomcat stench in most fruit-forward New World examples, including

Ontario and B.C. bottles, but they lack the aging potential of their elegant French cousins. In extremely ripe Sauvignon, the fruit notes become more tropical in nature. Papaya and passion fruit are common descriptors.

Sauvignon has been grown for centuries in France. The rest of the wine world has only caught on in the past two decades or so. New Zealand has led the charge and has become a leader in producing some of the more impressive Sauvignon Blancs in the world. South Africa is running right behind. Sauvignon Blancs from New World wine regions are gaining popularity with consumers because of their upfront and attractive fruit characteristics. A growing number of dedicated vintners in British Columbia and Ontario are falling in step with their counterparts in New Zealand, South Africa, California and Australia.

According to the Grape Growers of Ontario, 824 tonnes of Sauvignon Blanc was harvested in 2002. In British Columbia, the grape is gaining momentum as 384 tonnes were harvested in 2002. Although the varietal is well below other more traditional whites like Chardonnay and Riesling, the recent success of Canadian Sauvignon Blancs has more growers planting the grape.

The 2002 vintage produced a bevy of spectacular Sauvignon Blancs. The Vines panel awarded not one, but two Vines Awards. Both Peninsula Ridge Estates Winery and Vineland Estates Winery produced benchmark wines that would hold their own at any international wine tasting.

"In general, I think in Niagara 2002 was an almost perfect vintage for everybody," explained Jean Pierre Colas, winemaker at Peninsula Ridge Estates Winery. "I was a bit concerned at harvest that we had to prevent the sugar level from getting too high in order to protect the natural acidity. I prefer to have the acidity instead of high sugar levels to protect the balance and structure of the wine." His

FOOD PAIRING SUGGESTIONS
Oysters and scallops, Goat's cheese or Brie and other semi-soft cheeses, white fish such as pickerel or halibut, pasta with pesto or cream sauces. Sauvignon Blanc is also extremely vegetarian friendly. It's a zesty partner for vegetable risotto, mixed salads, vegetable skewers, or stir-fries.

wine showcases his deft handling of the fruit.

The success of Sauvignon Blanc in Ontario and British Columbia seems assured if the wines are simply made. Oak-aged wines, which are sometimes though, not always identified on the label, are called Fumé Blanc. This style of wine risk losing the bright and fresh fruit of the grape. Just as the lesson of subtle oak-aging was learned with Chardonnay, so too will domestic vintners tame the two-by-four thwack of their Sauvignons.

Tasting Panel: RD, KM, FG, WS, CW

VINES AWARD

Peninsula Ridge Estates Winery 2002 Sauvignon Blanc
Niagara Peninsula $18.95 (592303)
Consistency is the key when recognizing the talents of a winemaker. Winemaker Jean Pierre Colas has created a following for his Sauvignon Blanc — and it's well earned. The 2002 expresses generous notes of ripe gooseberry, lemon, and a hint of asparagus. The wine explodes on the palate with a rich core of acidity that carries the delicious fruit to the finish. Highlighted by a tangy ending that leaves the mouth yearning for more.

Vineland Estates Winery 2002 Sauvignon Blanc
Niagara Peninsula $12.95
Winemaker Brian Schmidt has crafted a perfect Sauvignon Blanc. Provided with ideal fruit, he has created a wine that typifies the grape's potential in Niagara. It opens with lush notes of gooseberry, lemon, and persimmon. On the palate, soft acids caress the fruit flavours of lemon and lime with an added touch of grass. Bright and refreshing, it's a beautifully structured wine from start to finish.

HIGHLY RECOMMENDED

Creekside Estate Winery 2002
Sauvignon Blanc

Niagara Peninsula $17.95

Another consistent quality Sauvignon Blanc performer, Creekside's 2002 has all the markings of a well-made wine. Opens with a burst of gooseberry, lemon, and fresh cut grass. On the palate, the fruit is given a lively push with an abundance of acidity. A bit tart on the finish, but when paired with fresh shellfish, it will shine.

Henry of Pelham Family Estate Winery 2002
Sauvignon Blanc

Niagara Peninsula $14.95 (430546)

In the ideal growing conditions of 2002 showing restraint with ripe fruit can yield wonderful results. Winemaker Ron Giesbrecht is superb at handling ripe fruit. Taking a page from the Sancerre style of Sauvignon Blanc, this wine showcases refined notes of gooseberry and asparagus with a fine streak of stony mineral. Crisp and refreshing on the palate, it's more about the balance of the acidity than the abundance of fruit. An ideal match for fresh oysters.

Puddicombe Estate Winery 2001
Sauvignon Blanc

Niagara Peninsula $15.95

This one is a hidden gem from the 2001 vintage in Ontario. Opens with classic freshly mown grass notes with traces of lemon and mineral. A rich core of acidity accents lemon and herbaceous flavours. Crisp on the finish, this fell just shy of the top award. A well-constructed and integrated Sauvignon Blanc.

Quails' Gate Estate Winery 2002 Fumé Blanc Family Reserve

Okanagan Valley $22.95

This is the best Fumé Blanc in Canada. This oak-aged Sauvignon Blanc won the panel over with its deep complexity and finely balanced structure. With one sniff, there's plenty of fruit including gooseberry, mango, and lemon grass and with a hint of vanilla. On the palate, there's ample acidity to lift the lush fruit flavours through to a fresh, clean finish. The added dimension of oak helps to soften the edges of the wine. A true display of winemaking craftsmanship, this Fumé Blanc is fit for any occasion that calls for a special wine – but keep it paired with seafood dishes.

RECOMMENDED

Château des Charmes 2002 St. Davids Bench Vineyard Sauvignon Blanc

Niagara Peninsula $12.95 (391300)

A restrained Sauvignon Blanc from the slopes of the St. Davids Bench located along side the winery. The nose is accentuated by ripe peach and pineapple with a sweet floral undertone. On the palate, soft acids balance the fruit and follow through to a crisp, clean finish. This one calls for a partner – think lobster or oysters.

Harbour Estates Winery 2002 Sauvignon Blanc

Niagara Peninsula $15.95

Leaning more towards a warmer climate Sauvignon Blanc, this wine opens with notes of melon, ripe fig, and pineapple. Soft acids round off the edges creating a lush mouth-feel. Built for those looking for a softer, gentle white.

Jackson-Triggs Okanagan Estate 2002 Proprietors' Reserve 2002 Sauvignon Blanc
Okanagan Valley $12.95 (593111)
Although this one doesn't burst out of the gates with typical Sauvignon Blanc characteristics, it has intriguing notes of ginger, anise, and mint with typical gooseberry and nettle. On the palate, it's a green salad of flavours highlighted by a balanced centre of acidity. A fresh clean finish tops a well-made wine.

Mission Hill Family Estate 2002 Sauvignon Blanc
Okanagan Valley $13.95 (118893)
New Zealand winemaker John Simes has done a wonderful job crafting lush Sauvignon Blancs in the more arid climes of the Okanagan Valley. His 2002 opens with voluptuous notes of melon, peach, and pineapple. On the palate, soft acids round out the tropical fruit creating a very friendly white that would be ideal on the patio or as a pre-dinner cocktail with shrimp.

Sumac Ridge Estate Winery 2002 Cellar Selection Sauvignon Blanc
Okanagan Valley $16.99 (731737)
A fine example of how to make an easy-to-drink Sauvignon Blanc. Opens with classic notes of gooseberry, lime, and hints of freshly mown grass. On the palate, it showcases the fruit with evenly balanced acidity which gives the wine a smooth mouth-feel. With its almost 14 per cent alcohol, it has a crisp, racy finish, which actually gives the wine an added punch. Built to be enjoyed chilled on the patio or on the dock.

Thomas and Vaughan Vintners 2002 Sauvignon Blanc

Niagara Peninsula $14.95

A stylish wine influenced by Sauvignon Blanc from the Loire. Opens with flinty mineral notes with lemon and peach blossom tones. A touch of residual sugar on the palate balances the acidity and helps to lift its pineapple and lemon flavours. It ends with a bright, crisp finish.

QUITE GOOD

Cave Spring Cellars 2002 Sauvignon Blanc

Niagara Peninsula $13.95 (529933)

A tightly wound wine with hints of leafy greens, lemon, and hints of stony mineral. Well designed on the palate with a zealous streak of acidity that gives the wine a tart finish. If you're serving fresh-water fish – give this one a try.

Lailey Vineyard 2002 Sauvignon Blanc

Niagara Peninsula $18

This wine has all the markings of a classic Sauvignon Blanc with peach, lemon, and nettle on the nose. On the palate, softer acids push the fruit toward a hasty finish. A well-defined wine that ends a bit too quickly.

Jackson-Triggs Niagara Estate 2002 Proprietors' Reserve Sauvignon Blanc

Niagara Peninsula $12.95 (618413)

A subtle wine that commands attention for the winemaker's deft handling of ripe fruit. Soft notes of peach blossom, green apple, and mint are revealed in this wine. Restrained acidity allows the fruit to gently roll across the palate. Ends with a crisp swish.

Mission Hill Family Estate 2001 Reserve Sauvignon Blanc

Okanagan Valley $16.95 (590349)

A highly floral wine that leans towards a softer elegance that would be associated with the wine's reserve designation. It opens with notes of lanolin and peach blossom with some pineapple character. Flavour profile includes pineapple, lemon, and honey with a touch of residual sugars that takes the edge off the acidity. Ideal for patio pleasures.

Peller Estates 2001 Private Reserve Barrel-Aged Sauvignon Blanc

Niagara Peninsula $14.95 (981308)

This lightly-oaked white is a simple sipping wine. It features loads of pear, peach, and vanilla. The oak softens the acidity and gives the wine an added depth that carries through to the finish. Great for the cottage.

Sandhill Wines 2002 Sauvignon Blanc Burrowing Owl Vineyard

Okanagan Valley $14.99 (587048)

A lightly-oaked wine that follows in the style of a Fumé Blanc. Features a touch of vanilla with lemon and a dash of spice. On the palate, it has a lemon tea character with an undercurrent of vanilla. Pair with smoked salmon or grilled vegetables.

Stoney Ridge Estate Winery 2002 Sauvignon Blanc

Niagara Peninsula $11.95

An attractive nose of ginger, anise, and asparagus gives way to a more subdued palate profile. With an abundance of acids, the fruit gets carried over the palate without a chance to strut its stuff. The lasting finish makes for a great wine to wash down salads and lobster cookouts.

Strewn Winery. 2002 Sauvignon Blanc

Niagara Peninsula $11.95 (582544)

A herbaceous white with grass and asparagus notes. On the acidity chart, it would hit the medium marker without enough fruit to make it a patio partner. Slightly tart on the finish – you may want to chase it with a shrimp or two.

OTHER WHITE WINES

If everyone were the same, the world would be a pretty boring place. The same goes for wine. A number of wineries and grape growers in British Columbia and Ontario are experimenting with non-traditional varietals. They plant small acres of little-known vinifera vines such as Viognier, Muscat, Chenin Blanc, Siegerrebe and others to see what the result will be in both quality and quantity. Sometimes the results are amazing, sometimes forgettable, yet if it weren't for experimentation, Canada wouldn't be producing quality vinifera table wines, or even Icewine.

In fact, most of Canada's early wine production came from experimenting with hybrid grapes. Hybrid grapes result from the crossing of two varietals in hopes of making a new grape that is adaptable to its surrounding environment. Due to the cool climate of Canada's wine regions, there have been many experiments that have produced interesting wines over the years. The best-known white hybrid in Canada is the Vidal grape; its hardiness and thick skin make it an ideal late harvest and Icewine grape.

So, we feel it's our duty to review the odd white wines—the ones that you may not see on liquor store shelves. This way, if you happen to stumble upon one on a wine tour, you can be the cool kid in the yard, setting the trend for others to follow.

Tasting Panel: LB, RD, TK, RP, WS, CW

VINES AWARD

Daniel Lenko Estate Winery 2002 Viognier
Niagara Peninsula $15.95

The little winery that could keeps churning out small batch wonders that are hard to come by. If you can get your hands on this French inspired wonder, you're in for a treat. Expressive fruit characters include freshly split kiwi, ripe pink grapefruit, and a hint of apple blossoms. Rich and delicious on the palate with ample tropical fruit flavours and a solid core of acidity, this one is worth the trip to Niagara.

Quails' Gate Estate Winery 2002 Chenin Blanc Family Reserve
Okanagan Valley $22.99

Chenin Blanc is a lesser-known grape that has done wonderfully well in France and South Africa. Quails' Gate has managed to capture the alluring qualities of the grape in this 2002 offering. Lush notes of grapefruit, passion fruit, and honey lemon tea give way to a succulently tasting wine. A natural sweetness up front combined with a rich core of acidity balance the wine's fruit flavours. With a little spicy heater on the finish, it's a gem of a wine that would be best suited for robust fish and Asian-infused dishes.

HIGHLY RECOMMENDED

Cave Spring Cellars 2002 Auxerrois
Niagara Peninsula $10.95 (500975)

Cave Spring is one of a handful of wineries in Canada working with Auxerrois. A grape native to France, this grape variety is suited to cool climate wine areas. This '02 is an easy drinking white with crisp apple and lemon flavours. Designed to be enjoyed in its youth, it's a supple wine with balanced acids and a refreshing finish. Built for seafood dishes.

Gray Monk Estate Winery 2002 Siegerrebe
Okanagan Valley $12.99 (321638)

The Siegerrebe grape is a German hybrid cross of Gewürztraminer and Madeleine Angevine. Gray Monk's 2002 offering captures the beauty of the grape's aromatic lineage with a bouquet that is very close to Gewürztraminer with perfumed rose water, ginger spice, and ripe lychee notes. Designed as an off dry, it's a lush, fruity white with enough acidity to balance the natural sweetness. Fantastic spicy finish caps a great wine.

Gray Monk Estate Winery 2001 Odyssey Pinot Auxerrois
Okanagan Valley $16.99 (620377)

The grapes used to make this premium white came from estate vines that were planted back in 1976. With smaller yields from the older vines, this wine is an intense portrait of a well-made Pinot Auxerrois. Attractive notes of peach, apricot, and nutmeg give way to flavours of crisp apple and peach. With a fine layer of acidity, this is a stylish white worth seeking out.

Lailey Vineyards 2002 Vidal
Ontario $9.95
A delectable wine with lush notes of ripe pineapple, melon, and lemon. Winemaker Derek Barnett has added a twist of sweetness that accents the tropical fruit flavours. Coupled with a great nucleus of acidity, this has all the zest and depth of a well-made Vidal.

Quails' Gate Estate Winery 2002 Chenin Blanc
Okanagan Valley $14.99 (391854)
This is another fabulous expression of Chenin Blanc. Highly aromatic with notes of freshly cut lemon slices with melon undertones, it even has a hint of grass. The herbaceous characters develop on the palate with a balanced acidity. Accented by green apple and pink grapefruit on the finish. A wonderfully made wine that would be a great addition fresh oysters or sushi.

Jackson-Triggs Okanagan Estate 2002 Proprietors' Reserve Viognier
Okanagan Valley $15 (593129)
This racy number has a distinctive nose – like a gin and tonic for those who imbibe spirits on occasion. With a full body from the high alcohol level, there's enough acidity to balance out the wine. A touch of malo-lactic fermentation has added a buttery finish to this beauty. A sexy wine for spicy foods.

Sandhill Wines 2002 Semillon
Okanagan Valley $18.99 (627679)
A noble varietal that hails from Bordeaux, Semillon is usually the silent partner in many of the finest white blends from the famed region. Winemaker Howard Soon has given Semillon, from the Burrowing Owl Vineyard, its own 155 case lot program to showcase its unique identity. A refined white, it opens with garden herbs, ripe

melon, and nutmeg flavours. There's a creamy
texture on the palate from some aging on its lees
and it's coupled with a good dose of acidity. It's
an attractive white that can really strut is stuff. A
crisp, elegant white that would be at home on
any table featuring shellfish, or light white meats.

RECOMMENDED

Angels Gate Winery 2002 Vidal Blanc
Ontario $11.95
An intricate Vidal that showcases the grape's
potential as a versatile table wine. Opens with
mineral, grapefruit, and tangerine notes. Crisp
citrus flavours with great lines of acidity make this
a great wine to be enjoyed with grilled freshwater
fish.

Calona Vineyards 2002 Sovereign Opal
Okanagan Valley $11.99 (364265)
The Sovereign Opal grape, developed by
Agriculture Canada, is exclusive to Calona
Vineyards. It comes across like a Pinot Gris with
its grapefruit and ginger aromatics. Designed to
be slightly off dry, it's a soft white with expressive
citrus flavours. A tad tart on the finish, but it would
be ideal with a fresh seafood salad or platter.

Cave Spring Cellars 2002 Chenin Blanc
Niagara Peninsula $15.95 (627315)
With grapes harvested from the Cave Spring
vineyards located in the limestone soils on the
Niagara Escarpment, this Chenin Blanc has
distinctive notes of stony mineral with grapefruit
and honeyed lemon tea notes. Slightly off-dry in
style, there are lots of tropical pineapple, kiwi, and
mango on the palate. Crisp acidity rounds out the
wine leaving a lingering, spirited finish. This varietal
is on the rise in Niagara.

Château des Charmes Wines 2001 Auxerrois

Niagara Peninsula $9.95

It's only fitting that the Bosc family introduced Auxerrois to Niagara. With founder Paul Bosc Sr. commitment to experimenting with grapes in Niagara, he has pioneered many of the lesser known varietals in Niagara like Auxerrois and Aligoté. Typical apple and lemon notes with a fine line of acidity balance the citrus flavours. A hint of mineral on the finish caps a wonderfully structured wine.

Gray Monk Estate Winery 2002 Kerner Late Harvest

Okanagan Valley $13.99 (158667)

Kerner is a cross between Trollinger and Riesling and in most cases, it comes across like a Riesling. Gray Monk's Late Harvest is more like a German Spätlese than a Canadian Late Harvest. It features lush citrus flavours with a dash of mint. Smooth and silky, its acidity keeps the sweetness in check. A great cocktail wine.

Gray Monk Estate Winery 2002 Pinot Auxerrois

Okanagan Valley $11.99 (096222)

An accessible white that would be a perfect match for Mediterranean-based dishes. Austere and crisp, there are ample fruit flavours like peach and lemon to make it a tasty, refreshing white.

Hernder Estates Wines 2002 Morio Muscat

Niagara Peninsula $14.95 (432567)

Another German crossing of Sylvaner and Pinot Blanc, Morio Muscat is known for its perfumed bouquet. Hernder's 2002 offering is wonderfully aromatic with generous notes of freshly sliced peach and apricot. Ripe fruit carries over to the palate with an added touch of ginger spice on the finish. With its oily texture, this would be a match for Chinese take-out.

Hillebrand Estates 2002 Vineyard Select Muscat Reserve

Niagara Peninsula $10.95 (291518)

There are few vineyards in Niagara growing Muscat, which is a highly fragrant grape. Hillebrand's 2002 reserve comes across like a Gewürztraminer with perfumed ginger, almond, and star fruit notes. A layer of sweetness is balanced by a crisp line of acidity that keeps the lush fruit flavours in check. Goes well with jazz and spicy Asian dishes.

Peller Estates 2002 Heritage Series Muscat

Niagara Peninsula $11.95

Another wonderfully aromatic Muscat with candied lemon, peach, and mint flavours. Luscious hints of pineapple and lemon with lots of acidity make for a crisp, delicious white that would be ideal for picnics at the beach.

Pinot Reach Cellars 2002 Bacchus

Oakangan Valley $10.95 (478495)

Bacchus is indeed the God of Wine, but it's also the name of a grape that has been created from Riesling and Müller-Thurgau. This wine features peach, pear, and apricot with lots of acidity. Although a bit tart, it does cleanse the palate. Try with spicy foods.

Reif Estate Winery 2002 Vidal

Ontario $7.95 (111781)

From the winery that has written the book on Vidal — from table wine to Icewine — comes a big, lush wine that features orange and lemon peel with slices of fresh peach flavours. With a touch of sweetness and a splash of acidity, it's a great value-priced white.

QUITE GOOD

Domaine de Chaberton Estate Winery 2002 Bacchus

Okanagan Valley $11 (953224)

This is a stylish white with a pinkish hue. Peach and lemon with some fresh almond combine with the lively acidity to create a great, refreshingly, crisp wine. Ideal as a cocktail wine.

Featherstone Estates 2002 Vidal Blanc

Ontario $9.95

An uncomplicated Vidal with highlights which include melon, vanilla, and mineral notes. A tad tart with a candied lemon flavour and crisp finish.

Harbour Estates Winery 2002 Vidal

Ontario $9.95

A fruity white that tilts toward the sweeter side of Vidal. Features peach and pineapple flavours with soft acids and good dose of natural sweetness. Best enjoyed on the patio.

Lake Breeze Vineyards 2002 Ehrenfelser

Okanagan Valley $12.90

Ehrenfelser is a hybrid cross of Riesling and Sylvaner that was developed in Germany in the 1920s. An early ripening grape, Lake Breeze's 2002 Ehrenfelser features lots of acidity that bounces its citrus flavours across the palate. Finishes with a crisp, hot zing.

Lakeview Cellars 2002 Kerner Morgan Vineyard

Niagara Peninsula $10.95 (535633)

One of the only Ontario wineries making Kerner, Lakeview' s features soft Asian pear, fresh green herbs, and grapefruit with a subtle sweetness on the palate. A soft white that's worth trying just to say you've had Kerner before.

Reif Estate Winery 2002 Trollinger X Riesling
Niagara Peninsula $14.95

This hybrid grape is a cross between the two grapes mentioned on the label. Ripe notes of banana, peach, and pineapple carry over to the palate with lush, supple flavours. Bright acidity gives the wine a racy, clean finish. Definitely a cocktail wine.

St. Hubertus Estate Winery 2002 Chasselas
Okanagan Valley $12.50 (436717)

Although not widely planted in the world of wine, the Valley has a few producers making wine from the official grape of Switzerland. St. Hubertus' Chasselas traits include cut grass with some lemon peel. There's a slight oily viscosity texture that gives the wine some needed body.

Thomas and Vaughan Vintners 2002 Vidal
Ontario $7.95

Crafted from old vines, this is a soft, lean Vidal with green apple and pear flavours. A little tart on the finish, it's a simple sipper.

Vineland Estates Winery 2001 Chenin Blanc
Niagara Peninsula $12.95

Vineland is another Niagara winery that has taken Chenin Blanc under its wing. Each year, its wine offers up a bevy of aromatics including lemon, lime, and a trace amount of garden herbs. It's a crisp, zesty white with some sweetness up front. Great for parties featuring multiple dipping stations.

White Blends

Why blend white wine? With the majority of New World wine consumers focussed on single varietal wines, it would seem to be fruitless to blend off two whites and risk confusing the wine consumer even more. Yet, in Canada there are a handful of producers who buck the trend by releasing white concoctions that are all over the wine map. Most of the white blends in this section are light on the wallet, with the exception of Sumac Ridge's and Vineland Estate's White Meritage, and they shouldn't be taken too seriously. Most wineries that produce mixed whites are generally creating easy-to-drink, no-thinking-required wines. Chill out and enjoy.

Tasting Panel: TP, WS, CW, AW

HIGHLY RECOMMENDED

Gray Monk Estate Winery 2002 Latitude 50
Okanagan Valley $11.45 (321646)
Named after the latitudinal location of the winery in the northern Okanagan Valley, this fruit cocktail has notes of peach, ginger, and even a trace of stony mineral. Elegance defines its structure with restrained flavours of apple, lemon, and peach. Ends with a spicy kick. Designed to be enjoyed in casual settings.

Thornhaven Estates 2001 Sauvignon Blanc/Chardonnay
Okanagan Valley $12.40 (725085)
Taking much of its personality from Sauvignon Blanc, this mouth-watering blend can be compared to a Jolly Rancher tropical fruit candy. Succulent pineapple, lemon, and star fruit give way to flavours dominated by fresh ruby grapefruit with a touch of honey. Balanced and crisp, this is a savory white for any causal occasion.

RECOMMENDED
Domaine de Chaberton Estate Winery
Chaberton Blanc 2001

British Columbia $9.90 (963462)

This value-priced blend is a racy white that features passion fruit, peach blossom, and apple notes. Grapefruit flavours dominate, but it's the crisp, clean acidity that gives this wine its appeal. A lovely wine to enjoy on the patio with a bucket of oysters.

Mission Hill 2000 Cordillera Okanagan White
Horse Canyon

Okanagan Valley $9.95 (574129)

Cordillera is part of Mission Hill's entry level VQA blend program that reaches out to price conscious consumers just getting into wine. The series of blends are named after areas surrounding the Okanagan Valley. This White Horse Canyon is a blend of Vidal, Riesling, Bacchus, and Gewürztraminer. A fruit forward white, it's a summer sipper with its citrus and fresh hay flavours. Fits into any budget.

Quails' Gate Estate Winery 2002
Chasselas/Pinot Blanc

Okanagan Valley $14.99 (585737)

Quails' Gate knows how to get the most out an odd pairing like Chasselas/Pinot Blanc. Designed as a summer sipper, it features apple, pear, and garden fresh herb notes. Pear and lemon on the palate and a good shot of acidity make this a wine destined to find its way to the beach for a feast on lobsters and shrimp.

Strewn Winery 2001 Two Vines Riesling/Gewurztraimer

Niagara Peninsula $9.95 (467662)

In a vintage like 2002 that delivered exceptional fruit, it's only natural that when two classic Niagara varietals are combined the result will be something special. Winemaker Joe Will's blend has ripe mango, melon, and peach notes. It's a refreshing, tropical fruit cocktail that is finely balanced. Its spicy finish makes this an ideal wine for grilled fish dishes or cream-based pastas dishes.

Vineland Estates Winery 2001 Rosomel Vineyard Reserve Meritage

Niagara Peninsula $49

In a daring move, Vineland has released a pricey white Bordeaux-style blend to complement its high-priced red Meritage. This one is a blend of Sauvignon Blanc and Semillon, although the Sauvignon Blanc appears to dominate. Opens with aromatic notes of freshly cut grass with squeezed lemon juice, and a hint of vanilla. With its robust palate, it's definitely a complex and layered blend with attractive flavours of pear, apple, and vanilla. Although it clocks in a close to fifty bucks, it's a well designed wine. Decant before serving.

Wild Goose Vineyards 2002 Autumn Gold

Okanagan Valley $12.95 (414755)

You can't go wrong with this tasty treat. Year over year, Wild Goose manages to release Autumn Gold with a flavour profile that is chalk full of peach, melon, pear, and pineapple. With a pleasing dose of acidity and its tropical fruit flavours, it's a white wine built for simple pleasures.

QUITE GOOD

Harbour Estates Winery 2002 Harbour Sunrise

Niagara Peninsula $9.95

An easy going Chardonnay/Vidal blend that
would be a good thirst quencher on a hot
summer day. Soft green apple and pear flavours
coast across the palate. A wine to chill with.

Peller Estates 2002 White Heritage Series

British Columbia $9.99 (582791)

Another simple white blend that would not be
out of place on a picnic or beach party. It features lots of orchard fruit including apple and
pear. Although a tad tart, it's a dry white that
could easily go with most quick-fix summer
dishes that don't require a grill.

St. Hubertus 2001 Oak Bay Vineyard Chardonnay/Pinot Blanc

Okanagan Valley $12.99 (513721)

The Chardonnay in this blend dominates with
pineapple and lemon notes. But, the softer acids
of Pinot Blanc offer a supple palate that controls
the tropical fruit flavours. One of the those whites
that you could cook with and sneak a glass at the
same time.

Sparkling Wines

There's a lot of sparkling wine made in Canada, including enormous vats of Baby Duck and other crackling pop wines made in bulk in giant wine factories. The presence of these so-called sparklers makes it difficult for producers of serious fizz to catch a break. But some estate wineries are staring down the stigma of Moody Blue and Baby Duck, which are more wine coolers than anything else, with exceptional sparklers that are as elegant and fun as the finest Champagne. For the record, only the French region of Champagne makes Champagne, everyone else makes sparkling wine.

Fundamental to the success of all good sparkling wines is a crisp, firm backbone of acidity, which can only be achieved in relatively cool climates. This makes Canada's cool-climate wine regions a natural choice for sparkling wine production. Vintners are using Riesling, Chardonnay, Pinot Noir, Pinot Blanc and Pinot Meunier to produce stylish and flavourful wines. There's even a few intrepid producers making sparkling Icewines, perhaps in an effort to add yet more opulence to what is widely considered Canada's luxury wine. (These wines are reviewed with the other Icewines in another section of the book.)

Two methods are generally employed for sparkling wine production. The Charmat process, or méthode cuve close, sees the wine undergo secondary fermentation in a reinforced stainless steel tank. The more rarefied méthode traditionelle has the second fermentation take place in the bottle in which the wine is sold. This is the quality method, which produces tiny pearl string bubbles in the wine. This labour-intensive process

FOOD PAIRING SUGGESTIONS
By any measure, sparkling wine is one of the most festive drinks on earth, a beverage to stir the spirits of any luxury-loving man or woman. Who needs food? That said, sparkling wine is as good a partner for food as many white wines. Although it's viewed as a apértif, its high acidity makes it a good match for fish, and delicately spiced Asian food.

means only small lots are produced each year. Some of the wines reviewed might be difficult for consumers to find because they sell out quickly, reappearing only with the next vintage.

Tasting Panel: TP, MS, WS, MS, CW, KW, AW

VINES AWARD

Henry of Pelham Family Estate Winery Cuvée Catherine Brut
Niagara Peninsula $27.95 (616441)
The second release of Henry of Pelham's sparkling wine production continues in the impressive wake of the debut 1999 vintage. The Niagara winery has abandoned vintage dating to provide more flexibility for future production, but continues the labour-intensive traditional method of sparkling wine production. Years of winemaking TLC have gone into this small batch wine, which offers a nice interplay of ripe yeasty/biscuit character and fresh apple fruit notes. This is a nicely concentrated wine with good intensity and poise.

Thirteenth Street Wine Co. 1999 G.H. Funk Vineyards Premier Cuvée
Niagara Peninsula $25

A deliciously creamy sparkling wine that will tickle the taste buds of even the most hardened I-only-drink-Champagne stick-in-the-mud. There's more Pinot Noir in this blend, which brings more structure, ripeness, and flesh to the party than the previous vintage. The wine is foamy, fruity, and fun on the palate, but with nice clarity focused on a core of crisp apple flavours.

HIGHLY RECOMMENDED

Hillebrand Estates Trius NV
Niagara Peninsula $21.95 (451641)
Made in the classic style, this sparkler has big complex flavours, including yeast tones with a core of apple and peach fruit. That plump core of fruit gives the wine a rounder texture, which is enhanced greatly by the wine's soft mousse (a fancy way to say fizz). Perfect for everything from cocktail parties to celebrating a win at the Montreal Grand Prix — though a championship bubbly like this is too good to spray all over the winner's circle.

Sumac Ridge Estate Winery 1999 Steller's Jay Brut
Okanagan Valley $24.99 (264879)
A cuvée of Pinot Blanc, Pinot Noir and Chardonnay, Steller's Jay is aged for a minimum of three years and is hand riddled and disgorged using the classical method. The use of Pinot Blanc adds some uniqueness to the wine, which is solid, with good biscuit aromas and spiced apple character. Steller's Jay's higher acidity makes for a racy wine that is just the thing to bring some magic to a dish with caviar.

Thirteenth Street Wine Co. 1998 G.H. Funk Vineyards Premier Cuvée
Niagara Peninsula $25
Nice leesy notes and intense caramel, toffee, and biscuit aromas herald the arrival of a world class sparkling wine. The complexity continues in the creamy flavour profile, which includes a range of warm bread and toffee nuances. The fizz dances in the glass, a winning approximation of a sea of pearls. The perfect companion for an elegant or romantic dinner party, it's also cheerful enough to open on a Tuesday night to share with good friends.

RECOMMENDED

Jackson-Triggs Niagara Estate 2001 Proprietors' Reserve Méthode Cuve Close

Niagara Peninsula $14.95 (563213)

There's nothing basic about the aromas of Jackson-Triggs' entry level bubbly. There's warm toast notes lingering in a waft of fruit cocktail aromas. The fruit carries over onto the palate, which is dry with a nice full body. It's fairly straightforward as sparkling wine goes, not that there's anything wrong with that. Drink now.

QUITE GOOD

Jackson-Triggs Niagara Estate 1999 Proprietors' Grand Reserve Methode Classique

Niagara Peninsula $19.65 (587691)

The nose heralds a serious sparkling wine that takes its cue from classic Champagne. The classical spirit animates the wine's frothy palate, which delivers nice fruit character and complexity from balanced acidity, nutty and mature notes.

Magnotta Winery 1999 Blanc de Noirs

Niagara Peninsula $14.95

Magnotta's vintage bubbly offers good character for not a lot of money. The aromas are subdued, but the flavours on the palate are full and rich. There's a tart edge to the short finish.

Magnotta 2002 Classic Vidal Charmat Method

Niagara Peninsula $7.95

A good time party wine, this off-dry fizz is extreme fruity with candied aromas and a sweetness to the palate. Too sweet for some panelists, this hit the spot for the sweet-toothes around the table.

Peller Estates Founder's Series Cristalle

Niagara Peninsula $17 (542142)

A serious style sparkling, Peller's Cristalle gains complexity and even more luxury from the addition of an Icewine dosage. The aromas are sumptuous: bread, baked apples, and other fresh fruit aromas. The addition of Icewine adds sweetness to the fruit flavours, but some tasters noted that it steamrolled the crisp, biscuity notes expected from classic fizz. A great brunch wine, served with fresh fruit cocktails and sweet and savoury baked goods.

Vineland Estates 2000 Méthode Cuve Close Riesling

Niagara Peninsula $18.95

It's little surprise that Riesling specialist Vineland Estates looks to the noble German grape to produce the cuvée for its citrus driven sparkling wine. Features steely and fresh aromas with some biscuit notes. The wine's flavours are very clean, with a fresh bracing acidity.

PINK WINE

ROSÉ

In Canada, summer is a season made for loafing – flaked out in a Muskoka chair with a pile of books and People magazines sprawled underfoot, with hints of Coopertone, retro tunes and grilled red meats in the air. Now is not the time for uncorking a prized bottle of Montrachet, Margaux, Mosel or Meritage. You want a wine that matches the occasion – something light and chilled with a burst of sweetness.

Like Panama Hats, convertibles and that special anxiety about losing weight before going to the beach, rosé is an integral part of summer. The days of drinking sweet, cheaply made rosé in the shade are fading as winemakers around the globe are crafting complex, elegant versions of this refreshing wine.

There are rosés for quaffing on the patio, rosés for sipping between bites of cherry tomatoes and seared steak and tuna, and rosés that range in colour from pale salmon to shocking pink. In

The range in rosé styles from crisp to sweet means not all rosés can be paired well with food. For a rule of thumb, if the rosé is labelled as "dry," "crisp" or "slightly sweet," it could be paired with grilled white meats such as chicken and pork or with fish. If the rosé leans towards the sweet side in style, it would best be enjoyed on its own or with a fruit dish—think strawberries and cream. Rosés are ideal for summer entertaining of all kinds.

seasons past, rosés have gotten the sommelier short shrift as big-spending oenophiles dismissed pink wines as overly sweet and cheap. The rosés featured in this section shatter the stereotypes.

According to Canada's leading wine educator, Linda Bramble, "rosés are the jewel wines, each with its own charms to be savoured drop by drop."

The opaque, pale colour is key to the enjoyment of these rosés which are continuing to gain popularity in Canada. Their hue and flavour depend largely on the production method and grape varieties used. One style has finished red wine blended with a finished white wine. The resulting colour is pink and the flavours are a complex blend of complementary characteristics. The more popular style comes from using dark-skinned grapes and limiting the amount of skin contact. The less time fermenting on the skins, the lighter the colour of the finished wine.

The result of both processes is a dry or off-dry wine refreshing enough to be enjoyed on the stickiest August day, but with the appealing red fruit characteristics found in red wines. So, as summer approaches, slap on some sunscreen, put on the shades and think pink.

Tasting Panel: LB, TK, RP, WS, CW

VINES AWARD

EastDell Estates 2002 Summer Rosé
Niagara Peninsula $9.95
This Vines Award winner also won the Barenaked Ladies Award for 'Best Rosé' at the 2002 Ontario Wine Awards. It's simply a benchmark wine for fans of refined rosés. Features lush notes of strawberry, maraschino cherries with hints of raspberry. The key to this wine is its acidity. There's plenty of it – but it doesn't get in the way of the fruit. The crispness enhances delicious

mouth-watering red berry flavours. A touch of sweetness balances the tartness making for a wonderful rosé that would be best enjoyed with grilled salmon and green salads on the deck.

HIGHLY RECOMMENDED

Gray Monk Estate Winery 2002 Rotberger

Okanagan Valley $13.95 (321620)

The only rosé in Canada made from the Rotberger grape which is native to Germany. Opens with attractive notes of Bing cherry, strawberry and cranberry. Built in an off-dry style, it's all red berry fruit on the palate. The off-dry character is balanced by a layer of acidity that carries the fruit to a refreshing finish. Great for sipping on its own or with a green salad with a splash of raspberry vinaigrette.

Harbour Estates Winery 2002 Harbour Sunset

Niagara Peninsula $10.95

A blend of Riesling and Merlot, Harbour Sunset succeeds because it's a quaffable rosé that finely balances the mix of acidity and sugar. It opens with a rush of strawberries. On the palate, there's sweet red fruit which is followed by a tart mid-palate highlighted by cranberry flavours. Finishes on a crisp note that leaves your palate refreshed. Best enjoyed watching the sun set.

Malivoire Wine Co. 2002 Ladybug Rosé

Niagara Peninsula $15 (559088)

Winemaker Ann Sperling has managed to craft some impressive rosés in the past. The 2002 offering is one of her best yet. Full of zest, it's an elegant offering that shows off the fruit without throwing it in your face. Opens with soft notes of raspberry and strawberry. The palate offers more red berry fruit, but the flavours are tied to a subtle streak of acidity. A fine wine that would be welcomed at any table featuring grilled fish – or even on its own while reading *Unless* by Carol Shields.

2002
ROSÉ PINOT NOIR

VQA NIAGARA PENINSULA VQA

ANGELS GATE WINERY LIMITED
BEAMSVILLE ONTARIO CANADA
PRODUCT OF CANADA ❀ PRODUIT DU CANADA
ROSÉ WINE ❀ VIN ROSÉ

750 ml   12% alc/vol.

RECOMMENDED

Angels Gate Winery 2002 Rosé Pinot Noir
Niagara Peninsula $13.95

Made from Pinot Noir, this rosé displays subtle notes of rose pedal with an attractive hint of cherry blossom. Built in a dry style, there's some heft to this wine. Intense red fruit flavours wash across the palate leaving a dry trail. Dry and light, this would be a fine match with medium cheeses or grilled pork chops.

Henry of Pelham Family Estate Winery 2002 Dry Rosé
Niagara Peninsula $11.45 (395897)

This is a stylish rosé that leans on acidity for its elegance. Opens with subtle notes of cherry and strawberry. On the palate its acidity draws in the fruit providing a crisp mouth-feel. Although a tad tart for sipping on its own, it would be an ideal rosé for grilled fish or shrimp – or try it with fresh oysters and a spicy sauce.

Sumac Ridge Estate Winery 2002 Okanagan Blush
Okanagan Valley $9.99 (136994)

Fragrant aromas and pure fruit flavours are the hallmarks of this delicious pink wine. It opens with crushed red berry, citrus, and lemon notes. On the palate, the fruit cocktail flavours are intense and well balanced. This is a clean, refreshing wine with a lasting finish. Good for the dock, deck or Thanksgiving dinner table.

St. Hubertus Vineyards 2002 Gamay Noir Rosé
Okanagan Valley $12.99 (507038)

Made from the Gamay Noir grape, this wine has the markings a great rosé. Opens with cranberry and red currant aromas. On the palate, it's all fresh red berry. A little light on the acidity, it lets the fruit tantalize the taste buds. It leans toward the sweet side of rosé, but it has got all the right moves to make you want more.

QUITE GOOD

Calona Vineyards 2002 Blush
Okanagan Valley $11.99 (627695)
A blend of Merlot and Gamay Noir, this is a beautifully extracted rosé. Red fruit of cherry, strawberry, and cranberry wash over the palate with a streak of acidity. A little tart on the finish, this is a perfect picnic wine.

Featherstone Estate Winery 2002 Cabernet Rosé
Niagara Peninsula $11.95
This featherweight rosé has a good dose of acidity making it a dry delight. A fair bit of red berry fruit finds its way through the wine, but it ends a little too quickly – just in time for another sip.

Harrow Estates 2002 Blanc de Noirs
Lake Erie North Shore $7.95 (489864)
A light offering that opens with notes of strawberry jam. Built in the off dry style, it has a solid core of acidity that helps lift the fruit to the finish. A pleasant wine that would be right at home on the porch.

Willow Heights Estate Winery 2002 Rosé
Niagara Peninsula $9.95
A lightweight pink highlighted by strawberry and melon characteristics. Hints of acidity give the wine complexity, but this one is all about the fruit. Ready to chill and serve.

RED WINE

CABERNET FRANC

Cabernet Franc is one of the noble vinifera grape varieties particularly well suited to cool climate wine regions and is considered by many vintners to be Canada's great red hope. The hierarchy of Bordeaux red wines puts the leaner, more herbaceous Cabernet Franc a distant second to the heavyweight Cabernet Sauvignon. If the two grape varieties were personified by 1980s soul rock duo Hall and Oates, Cabernet Franc would be John Oates, the guy with the mustache who rode Daryl Hall's coattails to stardom.

In actuality, it's another case of a child surpassing its parent. In 1997, DNA research confirmed Cabernet Franc and Sauvignon Blanc were the parents of Cabernet Sauvignon.

Cabernet Franc, whose buds mature more than a week earlier than Cabernet Sauvignon, is lighter in colour and tannins than its more fashionable offspring. However, it has similar or higher levels of acidity and similar flavour and structure. Like other Bordeaux reds, its flavours tend more towards the salad bar spectrum (most notably green pepper) than juicy red fruit. One can detect raspberry when it is under-ripe or over-cropped, although in warm vintages such as 1998 and 1999 the wine can showcase a layered fruitiness, which is extremely appealing.

The 2000 and 2001 vintages submitted for tasting were less than spectacular. In both British Columbia and Ontario, grape growers and wineries had difficulty with the grape in 2001. Although Cabernet Franc is a fringe noble varietal in the Valley as it's used primarily in red blends, Ontario has established the red grape as a perennial performer. The lack of consistency is a problem, but the early releases of 2002 show much greater promise. Still, there's no Vines Award in this category.

FOOD PAIRING SUGGESTIONS
Lamb, veal, beef tenderloin, London broils, venison burgers, grilled eggplant and portobello mushroom dishes, grilled vegetables, vegetarian lasagna, cheddar and other mild yellow cheeses, aged Stilton and Gorgonzola cheese.

According to Peninsula Ridge Estates winemaker Jean-Pierre Colas the key to crafting spectacular Cabernet Franc is simple. "I want to put the grapes in the bottle," Colas said. That requires a stern hand in the vineyard to reduce yields to ensure even ripening and the best possible grapes along with a deft touch with oak in the winery. "Varietal expression" is the watchword for Colas, who says there's no point in making Cabernet Franc if it doesn't taste like Cabernet Franc.

Frankly-speaking, the grape is better known globally as a blending agent than a one-grape wine. Adding Merlot and Cabernet Sauvignon helps fill in the holes of Cabernet Franc's lean structure to produce lush, mouth-filling wines. Cabernet Franc is the dominate grape in Cheval Blanc, which is considered one of Bordeaux's finest wines, and Viader, a California cult wine produced on Howell Mountain in Napa Valley. But the almost yearly success of one-grape Cabernet

Franc in Ontario and British Columbia is nothing to shy away from.

The biggest hurdle to overcome is marketing. When consumers hear Cabernet, they assume Cabernet Sauvignon is the topic at hand. Cabernet Franc produces truly great wines in France, particularly in the Loire and St-Emilion (Bordeaux) regions, but those are labelled as appellation or château wines. Only those wine lovers with a bit of Sherlock Holmes in them know what they are enjoying is premium Cabernet Franc.

The growing popularity of varietal Cabernet Franc in California will undoubtedly help cement the winning wine's reputation in the New World and help create a bigger market for these wonderful wines. Until then, consider yourself a pioneering force—the front line of Cabernet Franc fans who can reap the reward of being the first on the bandwagon.

Tasting Panel: LC, SP, VP, CR, GR

HIGHLY RECOMMENDED

Burrowing Owl Vineyards 2001 Cabernet Franc

Okanagan Valley $25

By the time this book comes off the press, this highly praised Cab Franc will be sold out. But, year after year, this one does exceedingly well in our tastings, and you may want to bookmark Burrowing Owl's web page to make sure you get a chance at the 2002, which could be just as fine as this one. Opens with an attractive bouquet of Bing cherry, mint, leather, and a splash of vanilla chocolate. Designed as a big red, there's plenty of red fruit in this hulking monster. Handcrafted from the vineyard to the bottle, there's no wonder this one is gobbled up by wine nuts.

BURROWING OWL
Estate Winery
Cabernet Franc
2001

Crown Bench Estates 1999 Cabernet Franc Vintners Reserve

Niagara Peninsula $19.95

If this wine were a line of clothing, it would be part of Juicy Couture. Chalk full of robust red berry fruit, slices of green pepper flow through the wine. Supple tannins and spirited acids make for a soft, chewy Cab Franc that has been woven together into a seamless gem. Uncork and let this one strut its stuff.

D'Angelo Estate Winery 2000 Viewpoint Estate Cabernet Franc

Lake Erie North Shore $11.90 (305862)

Although founder and winemaker Sal D'Angelo relocated to the Okanagan Valley in 2003, he left behind a trail of well-crafted red wine. This single vineyard Cab Franc from the northern shores of Lake Erie opens with aromas of cherry, green pepper, and chocolate. Leaning towards the mellow side of the tannin meter, it has lots of fruit flavours with vanilla chocolate, and some herbal character. An all round well built wine.

Magnotta Winery 2001 Cabernet Franc Special Reserve

Niagara Peninsula $11.95

Although there are no guidelines for labeling wines 'reserve' under VQA, this affordably-priced Cab Franc has earned its tag of special reserve. It has classic notes of raspberry, red currant and worn leather chaps with a hint of mint. There's a burst of red fruit on the palate with a touch of sweet oak. The fruit is lifted by streaks of acidity and soft layers of tannins. Decant for a while before serving.

Peller Estates 2000 Andrew Peller Signature Cabernet Franc

Niagara Peninsula $38 (981134)

Designed as a tip-of-the-hat to the founder of Andres Wines, Andrew Peller, this ultra-premium red is simply decadent. It abounds with classic Cab Franc character like Bing cherry, tobacco leaf, mint, and leather. There's plenty of oak, which gives the wine a sweet splash on the front and helps to soften the tannins. With an abundance of acidity, this wine will stand the test of time. If you are going to pop the cork, decant - but remember, this is an unfiltered red, so some sediment is to be expected.

Strewn Winery 2001 Cabernet Franc Terroir

Niagara Peninsula $18.95

A perennial high-ranking wine from Strewn, winemaker Joe Will has earned his stripes with the varietal. With grapes from the winery's vineyard, Will has molded this premium wine from the vineyard to the bottle. Opens with notes of freshly ground white pepper, red current, and sweet cherry. The flavour profile includes spice and red fruit, along with a hint of herbs. The wine really shines with its finely balanced levels of acid and tannin. Although a little firm in the finish, a little cellar time should soften the edges.

RECOMMENDED

Hernder Estate Wines 1999 Cabernet Franc

Niagara Peninsula $15.95 (399980)

With an abundance of quality red grapes from the 1999 harvest, Hernder has been holding back its '99 red monsters allowing them to age in oak and bottles for a few years. The result is a soft red with lots of flavour. Opens with notes of black cherry, bumble berry and cedar. A full-bodied red, it also features big oak flavours with red fruit and some herbal flavours. A classic Cabernet Franc from a hot vintage.

Hillebrand Estates 2000 Cabernet Franc Showcase, Glenlake Vineyard

Niagara Peninsula $40 (994582)

This single vineyard Cab Franc comes from older vines that tend to produce a naturally lower yield. The result is a wine with more depth and complexity. Opens with black currant, chocolate, and green tea notes. Fleshy on the palate, it is finely balanced with lots of cedar oak that should blend in with the dark berry flavours over time. A splash of sweet oak softens the tannins. Try with an excellent Italian dish - Osso Buco.

Magnotta Winery 2002 Cabernet Franc

Niagara Peninsula $9.95

Stylistically, it stood out in the tasting for its intense, yet different aromatics that feature red currant, freshly sliced green pepper, and a hint of violets. A subtle sweet hit with a finely balanced level of acidity sparks its red berry fruit. A perfect wine for those mid-week quick-fix dishes.

Mountain Road Wine Co 2000 Cabernet Franc

Niagara Peninsula $16.95

An upstart winery on the Beamsville Bench, Mountain Road has released an impressive line of 2000 reds. This Cab Franc would feel at home in the big red category. Rich plum, dark cherry, and green pepper characters dominate from the opening notes through to its smoky finish. Drinking well now, it would be a great match for beef stew.

Peller Estates 2002 Heritage Series Cabernet Franc

Niagara Peninsula $10.95 (582833)

This is a chewy Cab Franc. Built as an accessible red, this one has a definite soft spot. Opens with black currant, pepper, and green leaf aromas. It boasts a robust, yet supple mouth-feel with cedar, red fruit and pepper flavours. A tasty Cab Franc with a best buy tag. Try with spare ribs.

Pillitteri Estates Winery 2001 Cabernet Franc

Niagara Peninsula $14.95 (349241)

Just as Al Green softened the Memphis Sound with his seductively smooth voice, winemaker Sue Ann Staff has taken the Cab Franc grape and molded it into a smooth, sexy red. Tantalizing flavours of strawberry, raspberry, and a hint of mint combine with velvety supple tannins and crisp lines of acidity to create an approachable Cab Franc at a great price.

Sandhill Wines 2001 Cabernet Franc Burrowing Owl Vineyard

Okanagan Valley $16.99

Although the southern region of the Okanagan Valley is better suited for big, meaty reds, winemaker Howard Soon continues to show a deft hand at handling lighter reds from the area. This one hits all the checkpoints of a Cabernet Franc with a blend of red berry fruit and herbaceous characters. A hint of sweet oak takes the edge of the acidity, but there's a flash of heat on the finish. Take a chance with curry chicken.

Thomas & Vaughan Vintners 2000 Cabernet Franc

Niagara Peninsula $17.95

If you're looking for Old World comparisons, this one comes across like a well-built Loire-styled Cab Franc. Elegant and stylish, it features cranberry, red currant, and tea notes. The red fruit carries over to the palate with a layer of cedar oak. A touch of sweetness on the front gives way to a crisp, fresh finish. Think rack of lamb.

Tinhorn Creek Vineyards 2000 Cabernet Franc

Okanagan Valley $16.95

Tinhorn Creek only releases Cabernet Franc in years when they are able to fully ripen the grape. With this philosophy, this wine came from grapes harvested solely from its Diamond vineyard. The result is a wine that showcases ripe raspberry and cassis fruit flavours. Leaning towards light, it has enough acidity to make a crisp, fresh red without the tannins. Let it breathe for a bit before serving to allow the oak to soften, or lay it down for a few years.

Vineland Estates Winery 2002 Cabernet Franc

Niagara Peninsula $12.95

Another wonderful Cab Franc from the '02 vintage. Rich flavours include raspberry, bell pepper and a hint of vanilla and cedar. A touch of sweet oak with ample amounts of acidity and soft tannins make this a very approachable, consumer-friendly wine. Fifteen minutes in the decanter and this one will put a smile on everyone's face.

QUITE GOOD

Calona Vineyards 2001 Artist Series Reserve

Okanagan Valley $12.99

Although designated as 'reserve,' this is aimed at those looking for a young red that doesn't need to be swished around in a decanter. It features Loads of sweet, red berry fruit with a little dabble of herbs. Varietally correct, it's a consumer-friendly, value-priced Cab Franc.

Hainle Vineyards 1999 Knollvine Vineyard Cabernet Franc

Okanagan Valley $26.90

This organically produced Cab Franc is a little light, but it's fruity enough to be enjoyed on its own, or with grilled Tuna. Flavours include raspberry and strawberry. If you're looking for clean, organic wines, checkout www.hainle.com for more information.

Harvest Estate Wines 2000 Cabernet Franc

Niagara Peninsula $8.95

A consumer-friendly wine that leans heavily on the fruit. Features jammy plum, canned cherry with sweet oak flavours. Soft and approachable for easy quaffing.

Inniskillin Wines 2002 Cabernet Franc

Niagara Peninsula $11.95 (317016)

Designed to appeal to those with a penchant for Loire-styled Cab Franc, this is a light red with typical characteristics of sweet cherry, cranberry, and green pepper. A little tightly wound, it's a crisp red which should open up after spending time in a decanter. Calls for pork chops.

Lailey Vineyard 2001 Cabernet Franc

Niagara Peninsula $29

A dry, hot vintage in 2001 lead to more herbal characters in this Cab Franc. Green pepper, tea, and mint mingle with cherry flavours. Soft acids and supple tannins make for an approachable red.

Pelee Island Winery 2002 Cabernet Franc

Lake Erie North Shore $10.65 (433714)

As friendly looking as that tree-climbing fox the graces the label of this wine, this is an approachable Cab Franc. Aromas of spicy blackberry and sage spill into flavours of cedar, black cherry, and cassis which converge in a spicy finish. A great value red wine, just don't feed the foxes.

Peller Estates 2000 Cabernet Franc Private Reserve

Niagara Peninsula $19.95 (981209)

A little charmer that would appeal to those looking for a whole lot of fruit in their red. Jammy plum, black currant, and cassis flavours with soft tannins make for an accessible red. Goes well with Twister — just don't spill it on the carpet.

THIRTY

BENCH

Benchmark

2000

VQA   Niagara Peninsula   VQA

CABERNET FRANC
Steve Kocsis Vineyard

Red Wine • Vin Rouge

Thirty Bench Wines, Beamsville, Ontario
Product of Canada • Produit du Canada

13.4% alc./vol.   750 ml

Thirty Bench Wines 2000 Benchmark Cabernet Franc, Benchmark

Niagara Peninsula $35

This one has a bit of a personality conflict. Comes off as a cross between Pinot Noir and Cabernet Franc. More earthy in style, it features characteristics of Portobello mushroom, barnyard, and crushed cherries. Flavours are much the same. An interesting wine to try, but in a blind tasting, it's not benchmark Cab Franc.

CABERNET SAUVIGNON

In the world of red wine, Cabernet Sauvignon is afforded the same fanatical popularity Chardonnay enjoys over less fashionable white wines. Cabernet Sauvignon is the reigning heavyweight champion of the wine world. For many wine lovers, it is red wine to the exclusion of everything else on the wine list. We have California to thank for this. The surfer girls and surfer boys have turned the world onto one-grape Cabernet wines that deliver rousing fruit explosions to the taste buds. That movement has inspired many New World winemakers, including a strong Canadian contingent, to follow in their "go big or go home" wake.

But their Old World counterparts in Bordeaux continue to see the aristocratic grape variety as the King of Kings. Cabernet Sauvignon is the principal ingredient in their world-renowned blended reds, which often include smaller portions of Merlot, Cabernet Franc and a few other earthy vinifera grapes.

A hearty grapevine with particularly hard wood, Cabernet Sauvignon thrives in vineyards in British Columbia and Ontario. Surviving the winter is rarely a problem, but getting the late-ripening grapes to full maturity can be. In exceptionally cold and difficult years, the wines can be weedy and hard, but in fine vintages they are delicious and wonderfully versatile. The Vines panel saw the gamut of Cabernet Sauvignon styles in this tasting — from salad bar green to lush and fruity.

Like the French approach, the main use of Cabernet Sauvignon in both provinces is as a blending agent for Cabernet-Merlot or Meritage wines. But given beneficial growing conditions and in the right hands, it's not surprising that 100 per cent Cabernet Sauvignon wines are some of the best wines being produced in Canada. Classic Cabernet Sauvignon characteristics include cassis, red currant, mint, eucalyptus, black cherry, bell pepper and smoke.

Tasting Panel: LB, IS, WS, CW, JW

HIGHLY RECOMMENDED

Mission Hill Family Estate Winery 2001 Cabernet Sauvignon Reserve

Okanagan Valley $19.95 (553321)

The younger of the two Mission Hill Reserve bottlings that thrilled our taste buds, this struck us as an exciting wine fashioned in the guise of classic Bordeaux. There are savoury and spicy notes that tango around the glass with lovely blackberry and cherry aromas. The palate is fleshed out with nice smoky oak and vanilla notes, with some fresh cracked black pepper on the finish. This wine will improve in bottle over the next 24 months and will keep well beyond that.

FOOD PAIRING SUGGESTIONS
This full-bodied red is a superb match for most hearty meat dishes—everything from roast beef, lamb and veal to a wild kingdom of caribou and duck. Vegetarians need not despair; powerful Cabernet is also an impressive partner with vegetable stews, tomato-based sauces and mushroom risotto.

Mission Hill Family Estate Winery 2000 Cabernet Sauvignon Reserve

Okanagan Valley $19.95 (553321)

A seriously good Cabernet is obvious, like a great pop song or a great movie. Right from the first introduction, there's an "ah-ha" reaction. Everything fits together just so, without any exposed mechanics or extraneous limbs. Mission Hill's 2000 Cab is seriously good in the same way that Springsteen's Born to Run or the movie American Beauty is. It's round and smooth, with good structure, firm tannins and ripe fruit (particularly Bing and maraschino cherry notes). And like those other pop culture classics, this will age gracefully. Drink now to 2007.

Peller Estates 2000 Andrew Peller Series Cabernet Sauvignon

Niagara Peninsula $40 (981126)

This is a premium red worthy of the price tag. Handled as a small batch wine, this Cabernet Sauvignon showcases supple, velvety flavours of black cherry and cassis with an intriguing cigar box character. Although still showing the signs of oak, there's enough fruit and acidity in the wine to mesh the three when decanted or aged for a few more years. This is definitely the Cadillac of Cabernet Sauvignon in Niagara.

Reif Estate Winery 2001 Cabernet Sauvignon Estate

Niagara Peninsula $16.95 (304162)

This 100 per cent Cabernet Sauvignon offers full-throttle ripe fruit flavours (cherry, cassis, and plum) in a harmonious and smooth package. There's great intensity of flavour and extremely good balance here. Reif makes the most of 2001's warm harvest with this fully ripened and extremely tasty wine that will age nicely for up to 10 years. However it may be a titanic struggle to keep something so delicious around for any length of time.

RECOMMENDED

Creekside Estate Winery 2000 Marcus Ansems Signature Cabernet Sauvignon

Niagara Peninsula $25

Creekside presents a model of Cabernet that offers a marriage of Beauty and The Beast. Meaty aromas, which more than one taster described as "bacon fat," adds to the wine's beastly profile, while the plush, chamois-like texture marks the wine's elegance and splendor. This is a wine with good extract and complex notes that dress up the cherry and smoke character. Like any good fairy tale, there's a happy ending in the form of a nice fruity finish.

Mountain Road Wine Co. 2000 Cabernet Sauvignon Vintner's Blend Reserve

Niagara Peninsula $19.95

Another charming Cabernet with a blend of sweet and savoury notes, the debut vintage from Mountain Road Wine Co. features intense vanilla and spice packed around a core of red berry fruit. Judicious use of oak lends the smoky/spicy flavours a sweetish impression. This will evolve over the next 24-36 months. Enjoy with fully flavoured red meats or young cheddar and blue cheeses.

Peller Estates 2001 Cabernet Sauvignon Private Reserve

British Columbia $18.99 (618330)

Fruit from a single vineyard in the Similkameen Valley was aged in a combination of French and American oak barrels to produce this lovely wine with a luxurious suede texture. There's a range of different fruit flavours (mulberry, chokecherry, and cherry) on the palate that are balanced by a nice savoury/spicy component. An extremely well made wine; this will benefit from 36 months or more of bottle aging. Drink now to 2009.

Vineland Estates Winery 2002
Cabernet Sauvignon
Niagara Peninsula $18.95
A very clean and supple wine with ripe fruit flavours, Vineland Estates' young Cab makes the most of its straightforward package. There's not much in the way of complexity, but that blackberry and cassis flavour, which is enhanced by a kiss of mint, is hard to deny. Nicely balanced and mouth filling, this is a fine wine for sipping by itself or pairing up with lamb marinated with rosemary, prime rib or bittersweet chocolate desserts.

QUITE GOOD

Burrowing Owl Vineyards 2001
Cabernet Sauvignon
Okanagan Valley $26.90 (508200)
Surprisingly earthy and herbaceous style from one of BC's blue-chip wine producers, this has an abundance of barnyard, tobacco leaf, and meaty notes. The oak needs time to integrate. The acidity is elevated. These factors will sort themselves out in time, but the overall lack of fruit suggests drinking sooner than later.

Harvest Estate Wines 2000
Cabernet Sauvignon
Niagara Peninsula $15.95
A light and lean style of Cabernet that shows the cooler conditions of Niagara's 2000 harvest. Nevertheless, this delivers appealing herb and spice notes. The palate is lean with some tart cherry and vanilla flavours. Drink now.

Hillebrand Estates Winery 2002 Harvest Cabernet Sauvignon

Niagara Peninsula $11.95 (421479)

A light and smooth Cabernet with a drink-me-now personality. It offers some caramel notes with its raspberry and cherry fruit mix. Lighter in body and short in finish, this wine fits rock and roll's "here for a good time, not a long time" credo.

Hillebrand Estates Winery 2000 Showcase Cabernet Sauvignon Glenlake Vineyard

Niagara Peninsula $40 (994566)

A one grape Cabernet Sauvignon from a single vineyard, this medium-bodied wine shows nice complexity with its pronounced blackberry, mint, and chocolate notes. Not as rich and concentrated as previous vintages, the lean flavours are nicely spiced with white pepper and vanilla notes.

Kacaba Vineyards 2000 Cabernet Sauvignon Barrel Aged

Niagara Peninsula $22

A Cabernet with an extremely pretty nose, the lush chocolate, blackberry, and mint notes are very appealing. The flavours strike a more savoury note with tart currant fruit and leafy flavours. The wine's nice structure makes it a solid choice to match with a simple roast and beets.

Lailey Vineyard 2001 Cabernet Sauvignon

Niagara Peninsula $35 (591370)

A heavyweight Cabernet stuffed full of black currant and blackberry fruit, smoke, smoked meat and leafy/herbal notes. The concentrated and complex wine is made in an obvious big and brawny Old World style that divided the panel. Some loved the intensity of flavour; others were looking for riper fruit flavours. Fans of individual wines should keep an eye out for this. It will cellar to 2008.

Magnotta Wines 2001 Cabernet Sauvignon Limited Edition

Niagara Peninsula $18.95

You'll want to decant this leaner and lighter-style Cabernet to help blow off the funky sauerkraut and cat box aromas. Air will bring out the ripe fruit character and reveal the wine's true personality. Nice flavours and decent structure. Drink now.

Mountain Road Wine Co. 2000 Cabernet Sauvignon Barrel Aged

Niagara Peninsula $17.95

This smells a bit like a high stakes poker game: lots of meaty aromas like leather and cigar smoke. The wine has an impressive core of dark fruit to moderate those complex notes. It also features a good bodied and nicely integrated tannins. Drink now to 2005.

Peller Estates Winery 2000 Private Reserve Cabernet Sauvignon Barrel-Aged

Niagara Peninsula $19.95 (981183)

A nice 100 per cent Cabernet harvested from Niagara-on-the-Lake vineyards near Peller Estates showplace winery. Interesting chocolate and cinnamon spice notes hang above the bowl of the glass bringing to mind Juliette Binoche's out of this world confections in the hit film Chocolat. The flavours unite nice currant fruit with cedar and some tobacco notes. Good potential for short term aging. Drink to 2006.

Quails' Gate Estate Winery 2001 Cabernet Sauvignon Limited Edition

Okanagan Valley $18.99 (639617)

An attractive hint of strawberry fruit aroma mixed with eucalyptus and mint. The flavours hit the cherry and chocolate spectrum, making this a nice, elegant quaffer. It's a medium-bodied wine with nice structure. Drink now.

Strewn Wines 2001 Cabernet Sauvignon
Niagara Peninsula $19.95
This one is a nice expression of cool-climate Cabernet with tobacco, tea, mint, and spice aromas and flavours. The palate is dominated by dry tannins, which need time to soften. "A wine with potential" sayeth the panel.

Strewn Wines 2001 Terroir Cabernet Sauvignon Strewn Vineyard
Niagara Peninsula $37.95 (557082)
This one features a nice complexity from pencil shaving and cigar box notes. The palate is a little disjointed at the early stage of this reserve wine's development. There's some nice fruit on the front, spice in the middle, and grippingly dry tannins on the finish. The texture is nice and full — more so in coming years when the elements integrate and harmonize with bottle age.

Thomas & Vaughan Vintners 2000 Cabernet Sauvignon
Niagara Peninsula $21.95 (913749)
Winegrower Tom Kocsis used fruit from his estate vineyard to produce this flavourful red that is arrested by very dry tannins. Wild cherry and spice flavour dominates with some anise and mint aromas. Drink now to 2007.

CABERNET BLENDS

To best describe why winemakers blend red varieties, we decided to pull a buzzword from the business pages of the daily newspapers: "convergence." For some varieties, most notably Cabernet Sauvignon, Merlot, and Cabernet Franc, there is a synergy of flavours and structure that produce a better, fuller wine than any one-grape wine. The sum is, indeed, better than its parts. If only business leaders took a course in winemaking, convergence may have worked.

There is, however, no formula, no secret recipe for vintners to follow when blending red wines. Winemakers must sweat out the process, tasting every barrel in the cellar to produce their vintage wine. Bordeaux winemakers have been blending Cabernet and Merlot, along with Malbec and Petit Verdôt, for centuries, which is why some Canadian wineries refer to their red blends as "Bordeaux blends." The French figured out long ago that working with a variety of compatible grapes is the best insurance against disease and uneven ripening in the vineyard. The winemaker then has the flexibility to blend the harsh tannins and acidity of underripe Cabernets with the softer and richer flavours of Merlot, which ripens much earlier in the season. The percentage of each variety changes from year to year to reflect the strong suits of every vintage.

Like single varietal wines, blends vary widely in style, quality, and price. The range submitted for tasting spanned to the highest tier of Canadian wine, with many bottles priced at $35 or more. These are expensive wines to make. The judicious vineyard cropping required to reduce yields and guarantee the ripest possible fruit, and the expense of long-term aging in costly oak barrels, means that serious Bordeaux blends come with an equally serious price tag.

Be that as it may, it should be noted here that Canadian blended reds consistently outshine stand-alone Cabernet Sauvignon or Merlot. We hope that more wineries will turn to blending to make the very best big reds instead of focussing so much attention on stand-alone varietals, which need exceptionally warm growing seasons to thrive.

The process isn't confusing, but the wine labelling practice invariably is. Why are some wines labelled as Meritage (a California moniker for a Bordeaux blend wine, which rhymes with "heritage"), while some are Cabernet-Merlot and others still are given proprietary names such as Nota Bene, Trius Red or Oculus? Good question, and one that Canadian winemakers should address so the system can be demystified for confused consumers.

Tasting Panel: LB, BM, RP, WS, CW

FOOD PAIRING SUGGESTIONS

Blended reds offer a more diverse package for pairing with foods. Many of the wines reviewed in this section would be best suited for hearty meals. From stews and chili to steaks and roasts, most red meats would stand up to the blends. As well, some of the lighter blends could be paired with white meat such as pork and lamb. For vegetarians, try spicy pastas or grilled veggies with a nice hearty red.

VINES AWARD

Jackson-Triggs Okanagan Estate 2001 Proprietors' Grand Reserve Meritage
Okanagan Valley $24.99
Considering the fruit for this wine came from the arid desert of Osoyoos in the Okanagan Valley, it's no wonder this monster red comes across as a big Aussie red. Designed to showcase the fruit, there's plenty of blueberry, strawberry, and cherry, but there's also white chocolate. On the flavour side, it's all supple, velvety dark berry fruits with a solid core of acidity. A hint of sweet oak ties the fabric of this wine together. Drinking well now with some decanting, it should also age well for the next 5 - 8 years.

Mission Hill Family Estate Winery 2001 Oculus
Okanagan Valley $35 (572032)
Winemaker John Simes has developed quite a following with Oculus, which is the winery's premium Bordeaux-style blend. Every year, Simes manages to wave his winemaker's wand and out comes a magnificent wine. The 2001 builds on his past successes with its elegantly finessed design which showcases both depth and restraint. It shows notes of cassis and boysenberry with hints of cedar and new leather. Without going over the top on the oak, Simes keeps the wine crisp, bright and fresh with firm tannins and a great centre of acidity. This is a classic Bordeaux blend, and there's even a hint of Petit Verdôt to round out the wine. A true benchmark red blend. Drinking well now through 2008.

HIGHLY RECOMMENDED

Black Hill Estate Winery 2001 Nota Bene

Okanagan Valley $28 (708073)

A perennial favourite in the classic red blend category, Nota Bene comes from a small estate winery located outside of Oliver, B.C.. Winemaker Senka Tennant has developed a knack for crafting a wonderfully complex red blend. The 2001 opens with floral notes that develop into cherry and white pepper aromas. On the flavour side, it's sweet blueberry and cherry with ample amounts of tight tannins and spirited acidity. Although still in its infancy, this Nota Bene will age gracefully, or if you can't wait that long, decant for about an hour.

Colio Estate Vineyards 1999 CEV Carlos Negri Signature Cabernet-Merlot

Lake Erie North Shore $50 (612853)

This limited edition premium blend is a classic. Opens with shaved bitter chocolate, roasted almond, cinnamon, and blueberry notes. Flavours include dark berry fruit with a hints of sweet oak. Velvety and soft, this is drinking exceptionally well now. As one panelist said – 'simply opulent.' With only 100 cases produced, you may have to do a Google search to find a bottle.

Henry of Pelham Family Estate 2000 Cabernet-Merlot

Niagara Peninsula $24.95 (395855)

If you're looking for a complex, classic Bordeaux blend that showcases the talents of a fine winemaker, check this one out. Winemaker Ron Giesbrecht has taken fruit from a hot vintage and showed great restraint by keeping the fruit from going over the top. Opens with mushroom and forest floor aromas with some blackberry and cassis notes. But, the real beauty of this wine is found on the palate with its elegance. Finely

layered acids and tannins wrap around berry and cedar flavours creating a supple, yet crisp red that would be an ideal match for rack of lamb, venison, or even spare ribs.

Hillebrand Estates 2000 Trius Grand Red
Niagara Peninsula $58 (981050)

The master red blender, winemaker J.L. Groux, has done it again. The ultra-premium Grand Red is a classic Bordeaux blend with all the markings of a great wine. With only 40 barrels in production, Groux has been able to masterfully weave a red with ample amounts of cherry, black currant, and mint together with layers of crisp acidity and velvety tannins. There's even a trace of cedar ash notes from Groux meticulous barrel selections. This is a collector's wine — buy and save for a special moment.

Strewn Winery 2002 Two Vines Cabernet Merlot
Niagara Peninsula $11.95 (590109)

This one received high marks for its value versus quality. With this mid-range red blend, winemaker Joe Will has managed to extract a lot of complexity from the '02 vintage, which was cooler than '01 and 1999. Succulent red berry fruits with a subtle hint of sweetness on the palate add to the finesse of the body of the wine. Built to be enjoyed with food, this would be a fine addition to light meats like pork tenderloin or pork roasts.

2002
CABERNET

VQA NIAGARA PENINSULA VQA

ANGELS GATE WINERY LIMITED
BEAMSVILLE ONTARIO CANADA
PRODUCT OF CANADA ❧ PRODUIT DU CANADA
RED WINE ❧ VIN ROUGE

RECOMMENDED

Angels Gate Winery 2002 Cabernet
Niagara Peninsula $16.95
A finely crafted blend that leans towards the
Cabernet Franc side of the blending equation. A
core of green pepper and raspberry with a wisp
of black currant make up the flavour profile.
Merged with rounded tannins and bright acids,
this is definitely an accessible red. Throw into a
decanter for a while to let the oak blow off.

Hillebrand Estates 2000 Trius Red
Niagara Peninsula $19.95 (303800)
If the Grand Red is the Mercedes in the
Hillebrand red stable, this one is the BMW.
Opens with attractive notes of sweet cherry and
raspberry. A little softer than the Trius Grand Red,
it still has good tannic structure, bright acidity, and
rich, dark berry flavours. Another classic cool
climate red blend. Place in the cellar for 5 - 10
years, or decant for a while before serving.

Inniskillin Okanagan Wine 2001 Dark Horse Estate Vineyard Meritage
Okanagan Valley $25 (597039)
Another fine red blend from the Valley desert.
Opens with notes of sweet cherry, raspberry, and
vanilla. A little light considering the vintage, the red
berry fruit rockets across the palate with racy
acidity and soft tannins. Drinking well now.

Jackson-Triggs Niagara Estate 2001 Delaine Vineyard Cabernet-Merlot
Niagara Peninsula $29.95 (989269)
This premium red blend comes from vines owned
by Don Triggs, CEO and co-founder of Jackson-
Triggs Winery, and his wife Elaine. Although the
vines are still relatively young, in the capable
hands of winemaker Tom Seaver, this wine is very
elegant. Notes of green tea, mint, boysenberry,
and tobacco leaves point to the wine's delicate

nature. Although more brawny on the palate with chocolate, vanilla and dark berry fruit, it's the finely balanced acidity and tannins that make this wine special. Decant and enjoy.

Jackson-Triggs Okanagan Estate 2001 Proprietors' Reserve Meritage
Okanagan Valley $24.95 (597138)
This is a step down from the J-T Vines Award winner, but it's also built for those looking for a tasty red without putting out big bucks. Highlights include cherry and raspberry aromas with cherry coke and vanilla flavours. Designed to be consumer-friendly, this is one of those red blends that would be ideal for a dinner party of eight. You can keep inside the budget and impress the guests with a pleasing red from Canada.

Kacaba Vineyards 2000 Meritage
Niagara Peninsula $26
Kacaba pronounced [Ka-saw-ba], is another small boutique winery that is starting to make waves with its red blends. This one opens with notes of sweet cheery and green pepper with an earthy subtlety. Although there's a lot of oak on the palate, there's enough plum and cherry fruit to keep it in check. A medium weight red with crisp acids and firm tannins, this one should spend time in the cellar or in a decanter before it hits the tip of the tongue.

Kacaba Vineyards 2000 Cabernet
Niagara Peninsula $17
This medium priced red is more accessible than the winery's Meritage, and is no less delicious. Very attractive notes of coffee bean, black cherry and allspice. On the flavour side, there's ample dark berry fruit. Combined with velvety tannins and a good dose of acidity, this is one tasty red. Ends on a peppery note that completes the package. Savour with grilled meats.

Lailey Vineyard 2002 Cabernet-Merlot
Niagara Peninsula $22

This upstart winery led by grape grower-turned-winery-owner Donna Lailey and former Southbrook Winery winemaker Derek Barnett has released some exceptional wines from the '02 vintage. This beauty opens with anise, blueberry, and mint notes. It has got a firm body, but it's still approachable with enticing flavours of dark berry, toast, and vanilla. Tickle the tastebuds with this blend.

Mission Hill Family Estate Winery 2001 Cabernet-Merlot
Okanagan Valley $15.95 (257816)

When you get the ripe fruit, flaunt it and 2001 delivered the fruit in the Valley. This red monster features notes of plum, cherry, mulberry spice, and black pepper. Lush and supple on the palate, there's plenty of dark fruit and spice to go with the big tannins. Let this one out of the bottle for a while before serving with a AAA Alberta steak.

Mission Hill Winery 2000 Cordillera Okanagan Cathedral Ridge Cabernet Merlot
Okanagan Valley $12.95 (574087)

An entry level blend that makes the cut for its depth and quality versus price point. Opens with tempting aromas of freshly baked blueberry pie. The berry fruit with vanilla flavours dominate with an approachable mouth feel that features easy going tannins and lighter acidity. Think playoff hockey, pizza and Cathedral Ridge.

Pillitteri Estates Winery 2001 Cabernet Merlot
Niagara Peninsula $9.95 (349191)

Winemaker Sue-Ann Staff continues to craft accessible red blends that would appeal to most fans of medium-bodied reds. This one has an attractive floral nose with hints of strawberry and chocolate. A quick hit of sweet oak gives way to bright, crisp, red berry fruits with a chocolate, cedar finish. One panelist called it a lean, red machine. Don't wait to savour this wine, uncork it now.

Reif Estate Winery 2002 Cabernet-Merlot

Niagara Peninsula $13.95 (565713)

This is the best value VQA red blend in Ontario. Opens with lots of dark fruit, anise and vanilla notes. A hit of sweet oak is followed by ripe, lush black cherry, blueberry, and cedar flavours. Supple and soft without over oaking, this is a delicious wine. Buy it by the case and enjoy throughout the year.

Reif Estate Winery 2001 Meritage

Niagara Peninsula $26.95

Winemaker Roberto DiDomenico has created a wonderful premium red blend. Enticing aromas of chocolate, blueberry, and black currant flow through to the palate. With its velvety mouth feel and added flavours of peppery spice and plum, it's a tasty blend that can be enjoyed now, or in a few years once the tannins mellow out a bit.

Stoney Ridge Estate Winery 2002 Founder's Signature Collection Meritage

Niagara Peninsula $34.95

This is definitely a signature wine — one that has Jim Warren's fingerprints all over it. Founding winemaker at Stoney Ridge Estate back in the '90s, Warren has returned to the place that put him on the wine map in Canada. This classic blend features plum, blackberry, and blueberry fruit. Still tightly wound, there's plenty of tannins and acidity to make this a cellar dweller for a few years to come.

Summerhill Estate Winery 2000 Meritage

Okanagan Valley $40 (719856)

With a cooler vintage than 1999 and '01 in the Valley, it no surprise that this 2000 Meritage was thought to a be a Niagara red blend. Lots of bright red berry fruit with some minty notes pointed to fruit that didn't fully reach maturity. Dominated by Merlot, the flavours include candied cherry and strawberry. Classify this red as a lightweight that would be best enjoyed with white meat dishes or tomato-based pasta dishes.

Sumac Ridge Estate Winery 2001 Cellar Selection Cabernet-Merlot

Okanagan Valley $12.99 (551911)

Designed as a mid-priced, accessible Cabernet-Merlot blend, this one gets full marks for a hitting the target. Fetching notes of black licorice, Damson plum, and black cherry transfer nicely to the palate, with a full body complexity that starts with a sweet note and ends with a spicy flash. Perfect with a steak burger and fries.

Thomas and Vaughan Vintners 2000 Meritage

Niagara Peninsula $26.95

Since throwing open its doors a few years back, Thomas and Vaughan has hit its stride with remarkably complex reds. This 2000 opens with notes of freshly ground coffee beans, sweet cherry, and a hint of cedar ashes. A diverse palate of dark berries, garden herbs, and earthy mushroom give the wine a decidedly Old World nuance that goes well with its supple, yet restrained tannins. Still coming together, this a good example of a well-made cool climate red. Decant for at least a half an hour before imbibing.

QUITE GOOD

Creekside Estate Winery 2000 Laura's Blend
Niagara Peninsula $15.95 (572180)
Comes across as a meaty Pinot Noir with its
earthy, barnyard aroma. Sweet oak combined
with some red berry fruit offset the mushroom
and tobacco flavours, giving the wine an
interesting complexity. Built for big, meaty dinners.

Domaine de Chaberton Estates 2000 Meritage
British Columbia $23 (718544)
This one is drinking exceptionally well now.
Flavours include black currant, cherry, and vanilla.
A touch of sweet oak balances the dry tannins,
and there's enough racy acidity to give this red
some good length. Keep it paired with lighter
meat dishes.

Hillebrand Estates 2002 Harvest
Cabernet-Merlot
Niagara Peninsula $10.95 (287748)
An affordably-priced classic blend that offers
chewy dark berry fruit with a soft, supple
mouth feel. One of those wines to keep in the
kitchen wine rack for everyday enjoyment.

Hillebrand Estates 2001 The Collectors'
Choice Cabernet
Niagara Peninsula $15.95
A blend of Cabernet Sauvignon and Cabernet
Franc, this one leans heavily towards the
herbaceousness of the two red grapes. It features green tea and red currant notes with some
red berry flavours. Hits the palate with some
sweet oak and finishes with some cedar ash.
Drinking well now.

Inniskillin Wines 2000 Cabernet-Merlot

Niagara Peninsula $14.95 (627166)

A value-priced blend that has lots of bright, red berry fruit. A light weight in this category, it's best suited for delicate white meat dishes or as a picnic wine for a basket that includes an assortment of shaved meats and cheeses.

Lakeview Cellars 2000 Meritage

Niagara Peninsula $19.95

This one opens with an interesting sweet Port nose of plum, cherry, and brown sugar. The palate swings back towards a more classic Niagara red blend with red berry fruit and green pepper flavours. Heavy on the acids, but light tannins make for a wine worth enjoying in its youth.

Legends Estates 2002 Cabernet-Merlot

Niagara Peninsula $18.95

A crisp, firm blend that needs to find its way around before it starts to settle down. It has attractive raspberry and green pepper notes, but the fruit gets hidden on the palate by the tannins. Put this one in the cellar for a while, or at the very least, let it breathe for an hour or two before drinking.

Maleta Vineyards Estate Winery 2000 Cabernet-Merlot

Niagara Peninsula $11.95

An easy drinking blend that has enough fruit to please the palate. Hasn't been exposed to too much oak, so it leans heavily on the fruit and its acids. A good red to chill and serve on the patio.

Peller Estates 2001 Heritage Series Cabernet

Okanagan Valley $13.99 (582833)

A big chewy red blend that would appeal to
those looking for something that would compare
to an affordable Chilean red. Opens with wafts of
black currant and plum with cinnamon. Soft and
supple with cedar, plum, and chocolate flavours,
this is one pumped up red that would be ideal as
a house wine. Uncork and serve.

Peller Estates 2001 Heritage Series
Cabernet-Merlot

Okanagan Valley $14.99 (582858)

Another value-priced red blend that leans heavily
on the fruit. It has got lots of cherry, plum, and
chocolate flavours with a crisp, bright finish.
Looking for a tailgate wine – this should go well
with ribs.

Sandhill Wines 2001 Cabernet-Merlot

Okanagan Valley $16.99 (541144)

Designed to be hidden in the cellar for a while,
this one still needs to unwind. The red currant
and mint with smoky cedar flavours will only get
better once the tannins soften. Let this one gath-
er itself before pulling the cork.

Stoney Ridge Estate Winery 2002 Bench
Cabernet-Merlot

Niagara Peninsula $14.95

Although it is still finding its way, there's ample
cherry and plum flavours coupled with sweet oak
to make this one a mid-week charmer. Order the
pizza and decant while waiting for the delivery
guy.

Thomas & Vaughan Vintners 2000 Cabernet
Niagara Peninsula $14.95
A meaty red blend that features notes of mushroom, black pepper, and saddle leather. The palate is dominated by pepper with some tart cherry flavours coming through on the finish. A nimble red that could easy be enjoyed with smoked salmon or grilled chicken.

Willow Heights Estate Winery 2001 Tresette
Niagara Peninsula $29.95
Still in its infancy, this should evolve nicely into a stellar red. Opens with notes of chocolate wafer cookies, cedar, cherry, and red pepper. Flavours include sweet strawberry and red currants, with a garden herb finish. If the tannins mellow with age, this one should hit the mark.

MERLOT

Canadian Merlot has come a long way in a
relatively short period of time. A long succession
of lean and green 100 per cent Merlots had even
committed Canadian wine consumers questioning
the logic of making one-grape wines from such a
reluctant star. Such criticisms make perfect sense
considering Merlot has long been cast in
supporting roles. In France, Merlot is widely
planted, not to be produced as a single varietal,
but to support a rich blend of so-called Bordeaux
grape varieties, including Cabernet Sauvignon,
Cabernet Franc and Malbec.

Forever living in the shadow of the Cabernet
giants, Merlot counters the highly tannic structure
of Cabernet Sauvignon, and its supple fruit and
sweeter characteristics balance the Cabernets to
make a wine that is approachable in its youth.

On its own, a well-made Merlot can display supple fruit, such as black cherries, cassis, and raspberries, with a touch of sweetness. It has enough stuffing to handle oak aging, and if a deft hand is used in the process, chocolate and tobacco flavours mingle the fruit, giving the wine more complexity.

In Canada, Merlot lives a double life. The early flowering and ripening characteristics of the variety make it an appealing black grape to produce. Widely grown in British Columbia and Ontario, the grape is used by wineries as a blending wine and single varietal production. The consistent success of its blending capabilities can be witnessed in the Cabernet Blends section of the book. As a one-grape wine, the results vary widely.

Canada is now elevating Merlot to lofty heights. This year's tasting panel was once again pleased with the across-the-board quality, even with wines from Niagara's cooler 2000 vintage. There is a level of consistency starting to develop as the Merlot vines in Canada are maturing and winemakers are adapting to the vineyards with better results each year. Unfortunately, mature vines in Ontario took a beating from Old Man Winter in 2003. How that will effect the wine production is unknown as we go to press with this edition.

The jury is still out on domestic Merlot's ability to win an Oscar for a leading role. However, there are bright spots where Merlot shines, and an Oscar is an Oscar. An exceptional supporting role player is just as valuable as a bona fide star who can carry a film alone.

Tasting Panel: LB, DR, WS, CW

FOOD PAIRING SUGGESTIONS
The more complex, full-bodied Merlots would go well with red meats. The lighter-styled versions would be good companions with pork roast, duck, quail and other game birds.

VINES AWARD

Jackson-Triggs Okanagan Estate 2000 Merlot Proprietors' Grand Reserve

Okanagan Valley $22.99 (572040)

Just about any bottle of Bruce Nicholson's red wine production at Jackson-Triggs Okanagan Estate will give pleasure, but this is already gorgeous and particularly intense. Nicholson is doing for Okanagan Merlot what Jackie Kennedy did for the Chanel suit — establishing a bona fide classic style. This is a benchmark BC Merlot that is packed with sweet fruit while being smooth, almost plush in texture. Delicious.

Thirteenth Street Wine Co. G.H. Funk Vineyards 2001 Merlot

Niagara Peninsula $25

A massive Merlot sourced from a Niagara-on-the-Lake vineyard controlled by winemakers Gunther Funk and Herb Jacobs; this offers extracted aromas of chocolate, cedar, mint and cherry. Its serious nature is conveyed by a quick inspection of its intense, inky colour. The concentrated wine turns big and fleshy on the palate. It's packed with mixed fruit flavours that are focused by anise, pine, and herbal notes. The finish accents some aggressive tannins, but decanting it before dinner should soften them.

HIGHLY RECOMMENDED

Henry of Pelham Family Estate Winery 2000 Merlot Unfiltered

Niagara Peninsula $24.95 (291120)

The 2000 Merlot has a distinct varietal aroma with a touch of sweet herbs and smoke, which had tasters thinking this was an Australian ringer. Medium-bodied in the mouth, this is lush with good acidity for overall balance and a nice finish. It is a wonderful wine — with or without food — because of its approachability and spicy flavours.

Lailey Vineyard 2001 Merlot Estate

Niagara Peninsula $35 (591396)

Big and fleshy like Homer Simpson's belly, Lailey Vineyard's Merlot is a gentle giant. "Suede" was one taster's luxuriant description of this wine's complex profile and texture. There's a lot going on in the glass: tobacco, red fruit, vanilla, smoke, coffee, chocolate, and smoked meat (Mmmm… smoked meat, as Homer would drool). The finish is long and dry, thanks to some gripping tannins that will soften with bottle age. This will develop nicely over mid-term cellaring (five to eight years).

Quails' Gate Estate Winery 2001 Merlot Limited Release

Okanagan Valley $19.95 (639633)

Another smoky/spicy charmer that is packed with mouth-filling flavour, Quails' Gate 2001 possesses a core of earthy red berry and black berry fruit. This is a very stylish wine, with well-integrated oak and intriguing bacon, leather, and vanilla notes. Extremely easy to enjoy now, this is another affordable bottle with which to stock the cellar.

Sumac Ridge Estate Winery 1999 Merlot Black Sage Vineyard

Okanagan Valley $18.99 (593053)

This elegant, velvety-textured Merlot is a beauty. Refined and smooth tannins are backed by cherry and spicy fruit flavours, and peppery heat from the alcohol. Extremely tasty, this is drinking at its peak right now. An approachable sipping wine, the overall impression remains the winning combination of ripe red fruit and velvety smooth texture that coats the palate. Drink now.

RECOMMENDED

Burrowing Owl Estate Winery 2001 Merlot Estate Bottled

Okanagan Valley $24.90 (509885)

BC's Burrowing Owl lives up to its impressive reputation with this delicious and rich model of Merlot, with lots of positive oak, spice, and fruit character. It's spicy, licorice/minty notes add intrigue to the deep ripe blueberry flavours. The wine is elegant, yet thick and slightly confected in texture. Best enjoyed in the next two to three years.

BURROWING OWL
Estate Winery
Merlot
2001
Estate Bottled
VQA Okanagan Valley VQA

Jackson-Triggs Niagara Estate 2001 Delaine Vineyard Merlot

Niagara Peninsula $24.95 (989285)

A big wine that broadcasts the exceptionally warm 2001 growing season in Niagara, the inaugural Delaine Vineyard Merlot offers sweetish fruit with a vanilla and smoky oak character. The flavours are similarly rich and bold. The wine's obvious charms include its silky mouth feel and smooth red berry fruit on the palate. Decant for best enjoyment.

Jackson-Triggs Okanagan Estate 2001 Proprietors' Reserve Merlot

Okanagan Valley $16.99 (543876)

This sleek, quaffable model of Merlot is as stylish as the black label that adorns the bottle. Interesting graphite and clove spice notes blend with the subtle red fruit aromas. Fuller bodied, it becomes firm on the tannic finish. A good value wine to have on hand for the summer barbecuing season.

Mission Hill Family Estate 2001 Merlot
Okanagan Valley $16.95 (496109)
Plump and generous, Mission Hill's Merlot makes the most of its bright cherry intensity. There's a hint of cocoa in the background, which echoes beautifully as the flavours sweep across the palate. Highlights include its very pleasing texture and extremely good balance. This should develop nicely over the next two to three years.

Mission Hill Family Estate 2000 Merlot Reserve
Okanagan Valley $19.95 (553313)
A Merlot with great appeal, Mission Hill's Reserve is marked by a lovely raspberry character. Straightforward and focused on the palate, the wine is soft and smooth — an excellent wine to uncork when family and friends stop round. Expect to be asked repeatedly for the name of the wine you're serving. It's moderate in scope, but really quite tasty.

Nk'Mip Cellars 2001 Merlot
Okanagan Valley $16.95 (626416)
One of the highlights of Nk'Mip's impressive debut vintage, this presents yummy spiced plum flavours and a nice toasty oak note. There's good balance in this medium-to-full-bodied wine thanks to the clean, fresh fruit. The mouth feel is seductively supple. Drink now through 2007.

Peninsula Ridge Estates Winery 2002 Merlot
Niagara Peninsula $19.95
This nicely balanced Merlot seems to take its cue from France, with its nicely chiseled structure and savoury, dramatic character. It's no surprise considering winemaker Jean-Pierre Colas' career started in Burgundy. There's a depth of flavour on the palate, with chocolate, berry fruit, and mint notes in the mix, and a nice, vibrant grip-filled finish. The youthful tannins suggest this will develop with age. Drink now to 2009.

Quails' Gate Estate Winery 2001 Allison Ranch Merlot

British Columbia $12.99 (638163)

Soft, supple and generous, this Merlot stood out because of its distinctly floral aromatics. A lot of the wine's enjoyment comes from lingering over the bowl of the wine glass. The wine's plush texture puts some flesh around the vaguely blackberry and pepper flavours. The flavours are too subdued to serve this by the glass. Drink now.

Reif Estate Winery 2001 Merlot

Niagara Peninsula $21.95

A future star. This tightly wound charmer needs some time — maybe a lot of time — to reveal its full potential. There's earthy currant flavours and fresh mint notes that combine with the youthful tannins and cloak of toasty oak to possess a brilliant package. It strikes an uncanny balance between its elegant, refined frame, and the powerful core that will uncoil to reveal a classic wine. Drink now to 2010.

Tinhorn Creek Vineyards 2000 Merlot

Okanagan Valley $15.99 (530725)

Lighter and more astringent than previous Tinhorn Creek Merlots, the 2000 comes through where it counts, with a luxurious chamois-like texture and intense cherry jam character. An extremely well-structured wine, this wine presents its best side when paired with food. Barbecued red meat seems a natural selection, but if you want to keep it simple, uncork this with a nice chunk of fresh Grana Padano or Parmigiano-Reggiano.

QUITE GOOD

Arrowleaf Cellars 2001 Merlot

Okanagan Valley $16.95

This wine, with its cherry aroma and flavour profile, inspired a longish debate amongst tasters about the career of Neil Diamond. The debate rages on. Was he in fact a great American songwriter, or a hack who caught a break with less than inspired material? Are Crackling Rosie, Sweet Caroline or Cherry Cherry classic or cornball? Points to ponder as you sip this lively Okanagan Merlot.

Calona Vineyards 2001 Merlot Artist Series Reserve

Okanagan Valley $13.99 (458695)

A chunky wine that delivers tobacco and beet traits that are a bit more lively and appealing than one might assume from reading about a wine that tastes of tobacco and beet. Referring to the wine's lingering leather and pepper flavours might not help our case any either. Try it for yourself and see what we mean.

Crown Bench Estates 2000 Merlot Beamsville Bench Vintners Reserve

Niagara Peninsula $19.95

Herbaceous aromas and flavours of mint and green fruit mix with an intense loganberry are noted here. The wine's perfumed smokiness captivates — a bit like Mae West's come-on: "Come up and see me sometime." Don't put off that appointment for too long. Unlike West, this might not age too gracefully.

Hernder Estate Wines 1999 Merlot
Niagara Peninsula $16.95
Attractive chocolate, vanilla and blueberry aromas are the hallmarks of a well-made, softly textured Merlot that's ready to drink now. The sweet character carries over onto the palate and creates a nice full and rich red wine.

Lake Breeze Vineyards 2001 Merlot
Okanagan Valley $17.90
A little shy and retiring, this subdued Merlot takes a while to wake up in the glass and reveal its buried treasure: cherry, cocoa, and coffee notes. It has a nice full-bodied structure and smooth texture.

Lakeview Cellars 2000 Merlot Reserve
Niagara Peninsula $13.95 (565838)
A twist on the Donnie and Marie Osmond classic, this is a little bit funky, a little bit rock and roll. The graphite and tobacco notes that peak out of the wine's plum jam flavours aren't to everyone's taste.

Peller Estates 2001 Heritage Series Merlot
Okanagan Valley $14.99 (617654)
An affordable model of Merlot that spent some time mellowing in French oak barrels, Peller's Heritage Series wine impresses with its plush texture. The fruit flavours include some black fruit tending towards the sharp/tart spectrum. The wine's acidity is pronounced, making this a good foil for tomato-based pasta dishes.

St. Hubertus Estate Winery 2000 Oak Bay Vineyard Merlot
Okanagan Valley $15.99 (436758)
Mineral and sour cherry notes coat the tastebuds to make for a nice, but not tremendously Merlot impression. The wine's profile is leaner and more straightforward, making this a good go-to wine for Hockey Night in Canada with take-out pizza and wings.

Sandhill 2001 Merlot Burrowing Owl Vineyard
Okanagan Valley $16.99 (576751)
Smoky black cherry aromas compete with some earthy mineral, dill, and green olive notes. That earthy character carries over onto the palate, adding some oomph to the wine's soft and round profile. This is a great wine for grilled red meat that is only lightly seasoned.

Strewn Wines 2001 Terroir Merlot Strewn Vineyard
Niagara Peninsula $24.95
Here's a nice and bold Merlot that sets the scene with its sweetish red berry fruit and nice plump texture. It's nicely balanced but there's some alcohol heat on the finish. Decant and enjoy soon.

PINOT NOIR

Pinot Noir is the Robert Downey Jr. of the wine world because of its puzzling capacity for reaching the highest of highs and plummeting to the lowest of lows. It is a complete enigma for growers and vintners alike who are desperate to know what makes Pinot tick. The quest for the perfect Pinot has even led to the annual Oregon Pinot Noir Conference, which is one of the best wine conferences in the world. Often dubbed the Heartbreak Grape or referred to as winemaking's Holy Grail, this inconsistent grape variety is capable of producing the greatest wines in the world. But consumers have to kiss a lot of frogs before they meet a Pinot worthy of being crowned a prince.

From a winemaking perspective, Pinot demands a greater investment of time and money in the vineyard and at the winery, which is why none of the panel's recommended wines are what you would call cheap. For instance, Pinot Noir benefits from aging in new French oak, the most expensive wood barrels on the market.

Pinot Noir has been a grape that many wineries in Niagara have been nurturing over the years. The cooler climate and average shortened growing season has led many vintners to see Pinot as the "it" red grape that could challenge Oregon and Burgundy on the international stage. The Vines Award winner for Pinot Noir came from Henry of Pelham with its 2000 vintage.

"We've realized its potential in Niagara for Pinot Noir, and although it's difficult grow, it's the same difficulties around the world," explained Ron Giesbrecht, winemaker at Henry of Pelham Family Estate Winery. "We've invested in Pinot Noir by planting more vineyards, bring in lower yields, and hand harvesting the grapes. The 2000 vintage shows what happens when you pay attention to every detail."

"All the things that make a vintage difficult for other varietals actually help create the conditions for a good Pinot Noir," adds Giesbrecht. "The cool harvest season in 2000 allowed the Pinot Noir grape to ripen and it developed enough complexity which is important when making the wine."

Although Niagara is creating a buzz about Pinot Noir, Ben Stewart, founder of Quails' Gate Estate Winery in the Okanagan Valley planted Pinot Noir vines back in the late '70s as he saw the vast potential of the grape in the northern areas of the Valley. Since the early 1980s, Quails' Gate has focused on Pinot Noir. According to Stewart, the winery's approach is driven by concentration of fruit, cluster thinning shoot positions, clone development, and utilizing new technology. The 2001 Pinot Noir series from Quails' Gate is testament to Stewart's vision and dedication.

FOOD PAIRING SUGGESTIONS
The most food-friendly of the red wine family, Pinot Noir is happy served with most things available at the butcher shop: pork loin or chops, lamb, veal, steak, chicken and game birds, including pheasant and duck. It also pairs nicely with salmon, tuna, and snapper.

"The 2001 season had just enough heat for Pinot Noir, and with a cooler fall, it allowed us to pick the grapes at the exact right moment," he said. "Even with more research, we feel the best is yet to come, and Pinot Noir will continue to be our focus at Quails' Gate."

Classic Pinot Noir characteristics are strawberries, cherries, damp soil or compost, and barnyard or horse stables. Newcomers should know that the gamey or rustic aromas are more pleasant than they might seem on first sniff. But all Pinot discussions start and end with texture or mouth feel. Great Pinot is round with a velvety suppleness, and a deep penetrating flavour.

The grape's native land is Burgundy in France, which shares some climatic conditions with both Niagara and British Columbia's cool-climate growing regions. Canadian vintners are starting to produce some amazing Pinot Noir, often only in small batches that are snapped up by a cult following. Both regions are working to establish a benchmark from which consistently good wine will flow. That work is starting to pay off, as taster Linda Bramble noted, "These wines show we don't have to take a backseat to anyone when it comes to Pinot."

Tasting Panel: JA, CC, RM, CM, WS

VINES AWARD

Henry of Pelham Family Estate 2000 Unfiltered Pinot Noir

Niagara Peninsula $35 (268391)

Winemaker Ron Giesbrecht has crafted a benchmark wine that would stand shoulder to shoulder with any Pinot Noir in the $20 price point from around the world. The key to the wine's success is its complexity. Classic notes of dark cherry and raspberry with a hint of earthiness are indicators of a wine that has been

handled with great care. The palate features flavours of cherry and tobacco, but the clincher for the award is the wine's depth of texture. From its sweet fruit, finely balanced acidity and soft tannins, this Pinot has all the textbook elements that make for a wonderful wine. An outstanding example of how well Niagara can produce world-class Pinot Noir at a great price point.

HIGHLY RECOMMENDED

Creekside Estate Winery 2001 Pinot Noir
Niagara Peninsula $16.95 (572172)
The winemaking team at Creekside has established an impressive track record with Pinot Noir. Its 2000 took home the Vines Award last year and this one came very close to securing the top spot. Designed in the old-world style, there's plenty of character in this beauty, beginning with its notes of raspberry, hay and barnyard. Flavours of fresh cherry and raspberry with a layer of smokey oak are enhanced by a core of rich acidity. Round, velvety tannins make this a great, food-friendly Pinot Noir.

Malivoire Wine Co. 2002 Estate Bottled Pinot Noir
Niagara Peninsula $26

A small-batch Pinot Noir that captures the essence of the heart break grape. Deft handling of the fruit has resulted in lush notes of red licorice and cherry. Flavours include sweet cherry and cinnamon characters. The cooler 2002 vintage provided a core of acidity that's been perfectly balanced with the tannins. Bit of a heater on the finish.

Quails' Gate Estate Winery 2001 Pinot Noir
Okanagan Valley $13 (585760)

The entire Pinot line for Quails' Gate received rave reviews from the panel, and this 2001 limited release is definitely the best from the West. Influenced by the old world style, it opens with smokey bacon, black currant, and licorice notes. Flavours include cranberry, sweet cherry, and apple with layers of acidity and tannins weaved together creating a rich, textured beauty.

13th Street G.H. Funk Vineyards 2002 Pinot Noir
Niagara Peninsula $32

The master of Pinot Noir in Niagara, Gunther Funk, has worked his magic with this one. With attention to detail from the vineyard to the bottle, Funk's Pinot opens with notes of ripe cherry and raspberry with a touch of toasted bread. A velvety mouth feel accents the fruity flavours with a crisp streak of acidity. An earthy finish gives the wine an added depth of complexity. A fleshy Pinot that will stand the test of time.

RECOMMENDED

Burrowing Owl Estate Winery 2000 Pinot Noir
Okanagan Valley $24.90 (556613)

If you can get your hands on this one – count yourself one of the lucky few. As one of Canada's leading cult wineries, Burrowing Owl has made a habit of selling out of it stock quickly. This fruity Pinot Noir has notes of sweet cherry with a hint of topsoil. A sweet spark on the front gives way to a complex web of red fruit, tannin, and acidity. Fuller in body, this is a monster Pinot that will need time to unwind in the cellar or a decanter. Your quest is to find this wine.

Cave Spring Cellars 2002 Pinot Noir
Niagara Peninsula $15.95 (246561)
After some time in the bottle, this one will be a ringer. All the markings are in play from red currant, cherry, and earthy aromas. Flavour profile includes cherry, cedar, and tobacco, with some smokey undertones. Big tannins make for a big wine, but equally high acids manage to keep the wine in balance. Age or decant — either way you'll be happy.

Crown Bench Estates 2000 Pinot Noir Beamsville Bench
Niagara Peninsula $24.95
Barnyard, cherry, red clay – sounds like notes from a highly-priced Burgundy Pinot Noir. Earthy, coffee, and red berry flavours with rich acidity and soft tannins make for a versatile food wine. A fine example of how soil, location, and craftsmanship can make for a special wine. This is a small-batch operation, so quantities will be limited.

Daniel Lenko Estate Winery 2001 Pinot Noir
Niagara Peninsula $24.95
A tough vintage for Pinot in Niagara, but Lenko has managed to craft a fruity delight. It's a pot pourri of cranberry, red currant, and smokey oak. A sweet touch from oak accents the fruit without overpowering it. A little heavy on the tannins, but with its high acids, this should age well.

Inniskillin Okanagan 2001 Dark Horse Estate Vineyard Pinot Noir
Okanagan Valley $12.99 (530840)
This dark wonder is a complex blend of dark fruit with earthy characters. Although the desert region of the Okanagan Valley may not the best suited for fine Pinot, this one could make a case for its potential. Features cranberry and cherry aromas with a hint of leather. With a nice mouth

feel, there's enough ripe fruit with balanced acidity and soft tannins to make for a versatile Pinot. Features a little zing on the finish.

Mission Hill Family Estate 2001 Pinot Noir Bin 88

Okanagan Valley $13.95 (118844)
Sometimes simplicity goes a long way. This value-priced Pinot plays up the fruity side of the grape with generous notes of cherry and raspberry. Leaning towards light, there's red berry flavours with sweet oak on the tip with a spicy backbone. A quaffable Pinot for casual dining or just chilled on its own.

Quails' Gate Estate Winery 2001 Pinot Noir Family Reserve

Okanagan Valley $18.99 (639658)
A complex Pinot that borrows heavily from the Old World. Opens with smokey bacon, earth, and floral notes. A bigger red, there are plenty of tannins and enough acids to guide this one through the next few years. A touch of sweet fruit on the front adds to the wine's overall complexity. Needs a little time to breathe before hitting the glass. Will age gracefully.

Reif Estate Winery 2000 Pinot Noir

Niagara Peninsula $12.95 (282889)
An Old World styled Pinot Noir with notes of barnyard, raspberry, and cassis. A medium weight red, it features sour cherry, red currant and herbal flavours with rich tannins. Designed as a dry red, enjoy with succulent rack of lamb.

St. Hubertus Estate Winery 2000 Oak Bay Vineyard Pinot Noir

Okanagan Valley $14.99 (588954)

If you're looking for an easy-to-drink Pinot to unwind with after a hard day at the office, this one would do the trick. Highlights include its tasty sweet cherry, raspberry and strawberry characters. Light on the acids and soft tannins, it's built to be enjoyed now.

Tinhorn Creek Vineyards 2000 Pinot Noir

Okanagan Valley $14.95 (530709)

This is a lightweight Pinot with a big heart. It has the cherry notes while a hint of floral lingers in the back. Sweet fruit on the palate leads through a fairly balanced wine that leans on the acidity for its structure. A typical New-World style Pinot Noir with a spicy, crisp finish. Could be paired with white meats, or enjoyed chilled on its own.

QUITE GOOD

Angels Gate Winery 2002 Pinot Noir

Niagara Peninsula $18.95

A young Pinot that should weave together over time. Elements of red berry fruit with a hint of mint combined, with bright acids and firm tannins. A little crisp on the palate, but this should soften over time.

Cave Spring Cellars 2000 Pinot Noir

Niagara Peninsula $15.95 (246561)

This is one meaty Pinot. Classic notes of barnyard, cherry, and a hint of stony mineral best described the aromas of this wine. A fleshy mouth feel with firm tannins and a core of acidity make for a big Pinot that needs to spread its wings in a decanter. Definitely needs some food to shine.

Featherstone Estate Winery 2001 Pinot Noir
Niagara Peninsula $17.95
Young vines make for youthful wines. This wine
has lots of bright red berry fruit with a burst of
acidity on the palate. Light and airy, it's a wine
best enjoyed chilled.

Gray Monk Estate Winery 2001 Pinot Noir
Okanagan Valley $13.99 (251835)
For those who grew up with a mom that made
rhubarb pie, this wine's aroma should bring back
some good memories. With its basket of ripe red
fruit, it may not be a card-carrying Pinot, but it is
tasty.

Inniskillin Winery 2002 Pinot Noir
Niagara Peninsula $13.95 (261099)
From one of the pioneers of Pinot in Niagara, this
is a by-the-book wine for those looking to try
Pinot for the first time. Attractive notes of cocoa
and chocolate with lots of red fruit. The mouth
feel is much lighter than the rest, but the fruit
doesn't fall off. Finishes on a tart note.

Jackson-Triggs Niagara Estate 2001 Delaine
Vineyard Pinot Noir
Niagara Peninsula $24.95 (989277)
The first vintage from the ultra-premium single
vineyard owned by J-T co-founder Don Triggs
with his wife Elaine shows a great deal of promise.
For young vines, it manages to display classic old
world Pinot characteristics of barnyard, leather,
and red berry fruit. Lighter in style, there are some
tannins with a core of acidity that makes for a
refreshing red.

Kacaba Vineyards 2000 Pinot Noir
Niagara Peninsula $25
A youthful Pinot with raspberry, mint, and tobacco leaf notes. Lighter in style, there's enough fruit to make it an enjoyable sipping wine. A light red for those who lean towards whites, this would be a good buy.

Mission Hill Family Estate 2001 Reserve Pinot Noir
Okanagan Valley $17.95 (545012)
This one has elements of a classic Pinot with hints of tobacco, cherry, and raspberry, but it's a little light. In its infancy, tannins and acids are not getting along, but over time this could turn out to be a gem.

Summerhill Estate Winery 2000 Pinot Noir
Okanagan Valley $16.95 (446492)
A salad bowl of red berry fruit that comes across as light and breezy. Clean and refreshing with a nice finish.

Thornhaven Estates 2001 Barrel Reserve Pinot Noir
Okanagan Valley $14.95
An Ocean Spray mix of currant, apple, cranberry, and cherry. Light weight with bright acidity, it's a summer sipper.

OTHER RED WINES

Gamay Noir

Gamay isn't a global grape. It's getting terrible reviews in its French homeland, Beaujolais, where Gamay Noir is used almost exclusively to produce light and fruity red wine. Wine that a prominent French critic recently dismissed as being vin de poo-poo. Actually he used harsher language, but you get the point. The lawsuits are still flying back and forth.

But Gamay in a Canadian context is proving to be a different sort of wine than Beaujolais. Here it is richer, riper and even more appealing — consistently so. In the years since we started our Buyers' Guide tastings, Gamay has always been the most dependable panel tasting. The wines show well across the board. All of the other red wine varietals are much more variable.

There are a number of reasons why the Gamay tasting is more consistent than, say, Cabernet Sauvignon. The No. 1 reason is there are less wineries making Gamay, likely in large part because the wine is so unfashionable. But those vintners who make it know what they are getting into, which instantly makes for more care and attention in the vineyard and winery.

Canadian wine isn't going to make its mark on the world overnight, thanks to its ability to make seriously good Gamay. The reality is we're selling wine to our home market to consumers who will always be interested in enjoying a glass of seriously good wine.

Well-made Gamay is fragrant, supple, and delicious as well as plump and full — traits that every red wine drinker celebrates. Actually, make that wine drinkers in general, as Gamay has become a transition wine for wine enthusiasts. For many novice wine consumers, their journey of wine appreciation starts with light, fruity white wines and evolves towards the more complex and full-bodied reds. Getting from A to B would be a challenge if it were not for Gamay Noir.

Typically, Gamay is built as an expressly fruity, light-bodied red wine with low tannins and high acidity. The approachable style places the wine between the gentle features of whites, and the robust, bold features of reds. Since it is usually best enjoyed in its youth, Gamay also gives many wine lovers a chance to try a red wine without having to wait for it to mature for five years, or spend the big bucks on an aged red, although some Gamay's have been known to age elegantly for up to 10 years.

The fact that many Gamays are built to be unleashed early has often given rise to yearly celebrations in November under the banner of Beaujolais Nouveau or Gamay Nouveau. It is a fitting celebration as Gamay is usually the first red wine released from a vintage.

FOOD PAIRING SUGGESTIONS
Most Gamay Noirs are built to be consumed now. The fruity, light-bodied styles go well with hamburgers, tofu burgers and pizza. Grilled chicken and pork would also make for good companions. Some of the bolder Gamay wines built in Canada would pair with Christmas turkey, stuffing and cranberry sauce, dishes with Béarnaise sauce, or coq au vin.

In Canada, Gamay has found a home in Ontario. While a couple dedicated producers in British Columbia are working their magic with the grape. Like Pinot Noir, Gamay thrives in the cool-climate wine regions of Niagara and the northern Okanagan Valley. If you want to stage an inexpensive wine tasting, buy a Gamay from the list below and pair it with similarly-priced Beaujolais; and you can be the judge as to who makes the better Gamay.

Tasting Panel: LB, TK, RP, WS, CW

VINES AWARD

Thirteenth Street Wine Co. 2000 Sandstone Gamay Reserve
Niagara Peninsula $25
Ken Douglas and Erv Willms, winemaker and grower behind the Sandstone label respectively, are making the case for Gamay in Niagara. This is the version that other Ontario vintners are looking to better. It's more gamey than traditional Gamay, as it features a lot of oomph. It has got an amazing rich character, with cherry and raspberry fruit and complex smoke and vanilla notes. Absolutely stunning.

HIGHLY RECOMMENDED

Cave Spring Cellars 2002 Gamay Reserve
Niagara Peninsula $18.95
The biggest and best Cave Spring Gamay Reserve to date. The aroma is a little funky at first, but delicious black cherry and raspberry fruit notes emerge. That ripe cherry character carries over onto the plush palate, which is perfectly integrated and finishes nicely. There's a fine tension between the wine's firm structure and lively acidity. A great food wine.

Thirteenth Street Wine Co. 2001 Sandstone Gamay Estate

Niagara Peninsula $20

The 2001 Gamay Estate continues Sandstone's win streak with what can be easy called its signature wine. There's a lot of red berry fruit, smoke, and some mineral character on the nose, and a delicious core of raspberry/strawberry fruit flavours. Nice use of oak adds to the full, rich mouth feel. This wine tends to plump up a bit in the bottle and gain more complexity, so it's definitely a good cellar candidate to enjoy over the next six years.

Thirteenth Street Wine Co. 2001 Sandstone Gamay Reserve

Niagara Peninsula $25

Complex, complete, and utterly convincing, Sandstone's 2001 Gamay Reserve hits a high note for what is commonly a second-class citizen of the vineyard. It offers fruit-packed aromas, black cherry, and cassis flavours, and impressive intensity. Its smooth texture gives it sensual appeal, and the layers of rich fruit give it a complexity seldom found in the Gamay grape.

RECOMMENDED

Featherstone Estates 2002 Gamay Noir Unfiltered

Niagara Peninsula $18

A nice wine from The Niagara Wine Festival's 2003 Grape King David Johnston's Vineland winery. Featherstone's Gamay falls in step with producers aiming for a bigger, richer model of Gamay. This delicious wine is the opposite of traditional Beaujolais tastes: darkly coloured, richly flavoured, high in alcohol and dense, mouth-filling texture. Try it with turkey or seared tuna.

Henry of Pelham Family Estate Winery 2002 Gamay

Niagara Peninsula $12.95 (291112)
Henry of Pelham consistently makes a charming style of Gamay, so it comes as no surprise that the 2002 should exhibit textbook aromas of raspberry and pepper. It has cherry fruit on the nose and palate, and is a very pleasant chug-gable wine.

St. Hubertus Estate Winery 2001 Oak Bay Vineyard Gamay Noir

Oakangan Valley $11.99
A bright and fruity Gamay with pretty black cherry and plum flavours shaded with spice notes. Firm and focused on the palate, this probably isn't your best bet to sip by itself, but it would perk up a summer barbecue or picnic.

QUITE GOOD

Cave Spring Cellars 2002 Gamay

Niagara Peninsula $11.95 (228569)
This needs air to develop its full personality. Your best bet would be to decant before serving. Chokecherry, graphite, and smoldering oak notes dominate the nose. The fruit emerges as the wine develops in the glass. A nice affordable wine, with balanced acidity and good complexity for the price.

Château des Charmes Wines 2000 Gamay Noir Droit St. Davids Bench Vineyard

Niagara Peninsula $14.95 (582353)
Droit (a.k.a. Gamay Upright) refers to a clonal selection of Gamay, which Château des Charmes discovered on its Niagara-on-the-Lake vineyard site. It makes for a full-bodied, weightier style of Gamay, one with some tannins that would be enjoyable with grilled salmon, veal, or even cold cuts. The texture is soft, with enjoyable black cherry fruit and lively acidity.

Domaine de Chaberton Estate Winery 2002 Gamay Noir

Okanagan Valley $13.95 (721910)

This doesn't leap out of the glass in the same way that a more assertively fruity Gamay does, but its slightly perfumed cherry fruit flavours are bound to score points with family and friends. If this wine were a comic, it would be more in the Jerry Seinfeld understated and observational style than the Robin Williams hyper and full-throttle fashion — not that there's anything wrong with that.

Magnotta Winery 2001 Gamay Noir

Niagara Peninsula $7.95

Drinking well now, this wine is designed to be enjoyed within the next two or three years. Ripe cherries and spice flavours are brightened with a fresh streak of acidity. A great Tuesday or Thursday night pizza or pasta red to enjoy year-round.

Mountain Road Wine Co. 2000 Gamay

Niagara Peninsula $14.95

Ripe and rich, this is nicely pulled together so it's focused, with plum and berry flavours, and a touch of coffee spice on the finish. The debut vintage from a new Beamsville winery makes a nice first impression. Drink now through 2005.

Syrah/Shiraz

The French call it Syrah, the Australians call it Shiraz (rhymes with pizzazz), and in Canada, wine producers call it both. Talk about confusing.

The Aussies have made Shiraz wildly popular, and the grape variety seems destined to be the next big thing to rock the wine world. There's a lot of vines being planted in Ontario and British Columbia, so we're likely to see a spike in production a couple of years from now.

The appeal of Syrah/Shiraz in a Canadian context is its ability to fully ripen and offer vintners another full-flavoured red for their portfolios. "There's such a demand for fuller-bodied reds that Syrah, like Merlot, also an earlier ripening grape, has a potential to be a more consistent red varietal," explains Thomas Pennachetti of Cave Spring Cellars in Jordan.

Aside from 100 per cent Syrah, the grape seems certain to be blended with Cabernet-based and perhaps even Gamay wines to add some oomph to the finished wine. One Niagara producer, Peninsula Ridge Estates Winery, will launch its premium red wine Arcanum in 2004. A blend of Merlot, Cabernet Sauvignon, Cabernet Franc and Syrah, it replaces its Meritage as the winery's flagship red wine.

Winemaker Jean-Pierre Colas explains, "using Syrah makes things more flexible, adds more spice, more floral, more pepper. It brings something different to the blend. I know the potential and the potential is going to come."

FOOD PAIRING SUGGESTIONS
Gamy, meat stews or root vegetable stews, hearty mushroom soups, roasted pork loin or chicken dishes with tomatoes and garlic. The ideal setting for Canadian versions is the last barbecue of the season with a CFL game playing in the background, and the leaves turning vibrant shades of red and orange.

Tasting Panel: LB, IS, WS, CW, JW

HIGHLY RECOMMENDED

Cave Spring Cellars 2002 Syrah
Niagara Peninsula $17.95 (228569)
The second Syrah released by the Jordan-based vintner, this is a tremendous Rhône-style wine with big dark fruit and pepper flavours. It's not at all in your face or jammy, but it is packed with enough positive fruit and robust acidity to delight any red-blooded red wine lover. A supple yet elegant structure makes for an ideal food wine. Try with Cajun-style blackened fish or chicken in a blackbean sauce.

Jackson-Triggs Okanagan Estate 2000 Shiraz Proprietors' Grand Reserve
Okanagan Valley $19.95 (732172)
An amazingly ripe and generous wine, this B.C. red definitely is looking Down Under for its influence. It has the big fruit and nice spice elements of a premium Aussie Shiraz, with some firm tannins and sweet and savoury oak character from aging in American and French barrels. Extremely approachable and enjoyable.

RECOMMENDED

Inniskillin Wines 2000 Brae Burn Estate Shiraz
Niagara Peninsula $25 (558221)
A limited release wine stocked exclusively in some specialty shops, Inniskillin's second vintage of Shiraz is packed with fruit flavours and carries an attractive hit of cocoa. There's a lot going on with this flavourful wine, which was made by Australian winemaker Phillip Dowell. Nicely balanced with integrated tannins, it finishes with a lingering spicy flavour.

Mission Hill Family Estate 2000 Shiraz Reserve
Okanagan Valley $17.95 (585778)
Calling this Shiraz likely makes sense to the marketing folks, but the wine's personality leans more to the Rhône. There are lots of white pepper aromas and flavours, with some leafy, smoke and dark fruit notes. The panel reached consensus that this mouth-filling wine has good body and good typicity (i.e. it smells and tastes like a Syrah, er, Shiraz should). Only the firm tannins on the finish kept this wine from scoring even higher with our tasters. Drink now to 2006.

Mission Hill Family Estate 2000 Syrah Estate
Okanagan Valley $29.90 (556332)
Talk about confusion — a Syrah and a Shiraz from
the same winery. A rare offering from Mission Hill,
this Syrah has been aged exclusively in French
oak, unlike the Shiraz which spent time in both
American and French wood. Nevertheless a couple members of our crack panel were wondering
whether the same wine was poured twice
because of the similarities. In other words, there
are lots of white pepper aromas and flavours,
with some clove spice, smoke and dark fruit
notes. The tannins are better managed here, but
the wine lacks the core of fruit found in the Shiraz
Reserve. Drink now to 2007.

RED HYBRIDS

Baco Noir

If Bob and Doug McKenzie were wine drinkers,
they would probably uncork a couple of bottles
of Baco while watching Hockey Night in Canada.
Baco Noir is a hearty hybrid — hearty enough
even for Canadian bacon fresh off of the
Coleman stove — which grows very well in
Canada's cool climate wine growing regions.
Although not widely planted in British Columbia,
the robust red has been lovingly cultivated by a
few producers in Ontario and turned into a cult
favourite. It's like the John Candy of the wine
world — big, boisterous, unpretentious, and fun to
be around.

Cultivation and consumption of Baco Noir
(Baco, to friends) is to be encouraged. The
French hybrid is in no way the future of Canada's
winemaking industry, but it offers a decidedly
alternative wine to Cabernet. "Baco gets that
plush fruit character that's what makes it interesting. And, as it ages, cigar and cedar notes develop, which adds to its enjoyment," says Matthew

Quintessentially Canadian, Baco is best enjoyed with caribou, venison, duck, and even back bacon over the grill at the cottage. The best examples are also flavourful enough to enjoy by the glass, ideally in the fall and winter months. It is also an ideal burger, pizza, or pasta wine.

Speck, vice-president of viticulture at Henry of Pelham Family Estate Winery in St. Catharines. Henry of Pelham helped elevate the lowly grape variety into a vineyard star simply by giving it the same care and attention afforded to the leafy aristocrats, such as Cabernet Sauvignon, Merlot, and Pinot Noir. As a character in George Bernard Shaw's Fanny's First Play states, "No one is a king who isn't treated like one."

Proof of Baco's, and other hybrid vines, second-class nature comes from VQA legislation stipulating that even if the grapes are produced from a single, estate vineyard in Niagara, the label must carry the generic Ontario appellation. Unfortunately that doesn't help consumers separate serious and refined Bacos from the thin, acidic versions commonly produced by less painstaking vintners.

Henry of Pelham's Speck says the key to producing lush and flavourful red wine from Baco comes from reducing the crop down to one bunch per shoot. (The vine, he explains, generally produces up to four per shoot.) Less fruit means more sun and nutrients for the remaining grapes. Better grapes, better wine – it's that simple.

Tasting Panel: FG, WS, MS, CW

HIGHLY RECOMMENDED

Hernder Estate Wines 2002
Baco Noir Reserve
Ontario $15.95
If the finished wine arrives in the bottle with the same intensity and conviction that this barrel sample has, Hernder has got a winner on its hands. Big and bold aromas, particularly blackberry, smoked meat and leafy tobacco, dominate the nose and palate. It will take some time for that massive oak influence to integrate, but this wine is full and rich enough to handle the

extra weight. A great Baco for aging, this will dazzle your taste buds for the next five or six years.

Lakeview Cellars Estate Winery 2002 Baco Noir

Ontario $9.95 (307181)

This wine's dark colour announces the arrival of a serious Baco, an impression that is seconded by the wine's generous berry, pepper, and spice aromas. Full and richly flavoured, this is a plush, easy drinking Baco that is a benchmark for what this offbeat grape can taste like when it is well-made.

Mountain Road Wine Co. 2000 Baco Noir

Ontario $11.95

This new Beamsville winery is a welcome addition to the Baco club. This is a big, full-bodied Baco with lots of coffee and oak notes on the nose, and meaty, sweet fruit flavours on the palate. There's a lot of oak here, but there were little complaints from the panel. It's a bold enough wine to be able to withstand the walloping two-by-four effect. That mocha note returns on the palate. An impressive debut.

RECOMMENDED

Harvest Estate Wines 2000 Baco Noir

Ontario $8.95 (579979)

Judicious use of oak aging has plumped up the flavour profile of this ripe and robust Baco. The nose features toast, smoke, and some black fruit notes that carry over onto the palate. There's also some black licorice and floral notes found on the lingering finish. An excellent value food wine, this would pair nicely with barbecued meat, pasta dishes with roasted tomato and grilled vegetable sauces or a four cheese pizza.

Henry of Pelham Family Estate Winery 2002 Baco Noir

Ontario $12.25 (270926)

Ontario's stellar 2002 harvest even benefited Baco, adding a delicious core of fruit to the palate of what can easily be a leaner-style red wine. This smooth and well-balanced wine offers a medley of ripe red fruit and savoury oak spice notes. Ready for drinking now, this will age for three to five years. Why wait? Drink now with rustic dishes, such as venison sausages or pot roast.

Hernder Estate Wines 2000 Baco Noir

Ontario $10.95

Another ripe and robust expression of Baco that has been plumped up by oak aging. Aromas of black fruit, toast, and smoke are mirrored by the flavours on the palate. Nice soft structure, with some anise notes on the lingering finish. Good value wine to stock as your house wine.

Legends Estate Winery 2002 Baco Noir

Ontario $9.65

Welcome a new addition to Team Baco. This Beamsville winery presents a nice medium bodied model with bright cassis and berry fruit. The palate is round and smooth, balanced by bright acidity and intensity of flavour. Excellent food wine.

Peller Estates Winery 2002 Heritage Series Baco Noir

Ontario $10.95 (582841)

Nice cherry and cassis fruit are featured in this value-priced Baco, which has a subtle cedar edge to it. The oak helps to temper the wine's tart acidity and herbal elements. Consider chilling for 15 minutes prior to serving with a simple pasta dish.

QUITE GOOD

Ancient Coast 2002 Baco Noir
Ontario $8.50 (55918)
Raspberry and vanilla flavours dominate the
palate of this small stature Baco. The higher
acidity and tart fruit notes make this more of a
dinnertime wine. That brightness would be a
good contrast for hearty stew or veal Parmesan.

Pelee Island Winery 2002 Baco Noir
Ontario $7.95 (485128)
This is a bright Baco that is extremely popular with
fans of Pelee Island Winery. There's some spice
notes hanging around with the red raspberry fruit.
Good expression of Baco's party personality that
would add some sizzle to weekday pasta or
burger nights.

Summerhill Pyramid Winery 2002 Baco Noir
Okanagan Valley $19.95
There's a decidedly sweet hit to the ripe fruit
flavours found in our lone B.C. Baco. The flavour
is a bit candied, but the wine is balanced. A great
porch quaffer or free-spirited partner for pizza
and pasta night.

Maréchal Foch

Another French hybrid cultivated by a handful
of die-hards, Maréchal Foch thrives when it is
reduced to low yields in the vineyards and
treated to a lengthy stint mellowing out in newer
oak barrels — even wines respond to the luxury
pampering of a spa treatment.

Maréchal Foch (or plain old Foch) is a
winter-hardy vine, and winemakers can count on
the grapes reaching their full potential year after
year. Although not widely popular with wine
aficionados, it has its loyal followers. There are a
few wineries in Ontario and British Columbia

FOOD PAIRING SUGGESTIONS
Mushroom-based dishes
and gamey meats, such
as venison, rabbit and
duck. It would also
partner with other hearty
foods, including lentil or
beef stew and barbe-
cued meats.

making Foch, fewer still affording it the full service treatment to produce the finest possible Foch. Lucky for intrepid winos, the premium producers aren't hard to track down.

Tasting Panel: FG, WS, TK, CW

VINES AWARD

Malivoire Wine Co. 2002 Old Vines Foch

Ontario $22 (551036)

Malivoire's Old Vines Foch is a consistently stellar wine, with all the drama of Cinderella: lowly servant girl is whisked to the ball where she intoxicates Prince Charming. In this case, winemaker Ann Sperling dresses up lowly Foch in all the finery usually reserved for Cabernet or Pinot. The result? Be still our hearts. One of the best expressions of Foch yet produced, this offers an intense cherry note with some smoked meat and leather notes, and sweetish oak spice. Approachable now, this has the stuffing to age for five years or longer.

HIGHLY RECOMMENDED

Thomas and Vaughan Vintners 2002 Maréchal Foch

Ontario $14.95

Thomas and Vaughan Vintners has a winning way with Foch. The Beamsville winery routinely turns its estate fruit into smokey, sweetly flavoured wines that are crowd-pleasers. The 2002 vintage has that plump core of fruit that make wines total knockouts. A lovely silky texture enhances the tasting experience. Well done.

RECOMMENDED

Quails' Gate Estate Winery 2001 Old Vines Foch Limited Release
Okanagan Valley $19.99 (411348)

Quails' Gate's Foch is one of the cult wines of B.C., with a loyal following that snaps up its allotment in short order. The new vintage is soft and pleasant, with complex tobacco and mocha vanilla notes behind the cassis fruit. The middle palate and finish are lean and dry, not quite what you expect from the spicy aromas.

QUITE GOOD

Caroline Cellars Winery 2001 Maréchal Foch
Ontario $8.95

The debut vintage from a new Niagara-on-the-Lake winery offers the nice red fruit typically associated with Foch while some leafy/herbal notes add some interest to the aromas and flavour profile. This is a lighter style Foch that has bright acidity and good balance. Drink now.

Mountain Road Wine Co. 2000 Maréchal Foch
Ontario $12.95

A model of M-Fo (hey, if it works for J-Lo, why not?) that's a full-on oak bomb. There's a lot of savoury oak coating the red fruit, adding some coconut and vanilla flavours to the profile. One taster thought it was a bit over-the-top, but others were more forgiving. It's full-flavoured with a round texture, and bound to draw some attention to this newly-opened Beamsville winery.

St. Hubertus Estate Winery 2002 Oak Bay Vineyard Maréchal Foch

Okanagan Valley $14.99

Rich and jammy, St. Hubertus Estate makes a version of Foch that makes friends extremely easily. The emphasis is on the polished plummy flavours, while the finish turns leafy with some tobacco and bell pepper flavours. Best with food.

Summerhill Pyramid Winery 2001 Foch Solus Enchanted Vines

British Columbia $19.95

The label of this striking wine looks like the cover for an L. Ron Hubbard fantasy novel, and it's easy to imagine that the founder of the Church of Scientology would appreciate the Enchanted Vines moniker attached to this organic wine. Wine lovers of all stripes will appreciate the plummy fruit flavours and smooth texture. Drink now.

DESSERT WINE

Icewine. The sweet nectar of the gods. The golden honey of wine. Whatever you want to call it, Icewine is sweet, seductive, and expensive. It's a rare and elegant wine unlike any other. It's made from frozen grapes that have been left on the vine for late harvest, usually in December and January. According to Canadian Icewine standards set by the VQA, Icewine grapes can only be harvested after the temperature reaches -8°C or colder. The grapes are pressed immediately while still frozen. The yields for such grapes are only 75 to 100 litres of intensely flavoured juice per tonne of grapes. The result is a higher priced wine due to the vastly reduced volume of juice per tonne.

To craft an exquisite Icewine, the winemaker must balance the highly concentrated sugar levels with the low acidity of the juice. An Icewine without balanced acidity is pancake syrup. Well-made vintages are sweet, but never cloying. With each passing vintage, winemakers are beginning to hit the balanced mark on a regular basis.

Through a number of international wine competitions, including the prestigious VinExpo in France and VinItaly in Italy, Canadian Icewine has helped place Canadian wines on the world stage. The two most popular grapes for Canadian Icewine are Riesling and Vidal. In Ontario, the hardy Vidal grape was the first to be successfully turned into Icewine. Its thick skin makes it ideal for allowing the grape juice to freeze without splitting open and losing valuable liquid. Although Vidal is not as abundant in British Columbia, Riesling has become a popular alternative in the Icewine arena. In both Ontario and British Columbia, many producers are crafting dazzling Riesling Icewines.

As the popularity of Icewine grows around the world, winemakers are continuing to experiment with different varieties in the hopes of creating more rare and exotic vintages. Vintages of Chardonnay, Gewürztraminer, Pinot Gris, Pinot Blanc, Ehrenfelser and red viniferas like Cabernet Franc, Pinot Noir, Merlot and even Cabernet Sauvignon all made appearances in our exhaustive tasting.

The fruit for the 2000 vintage in both British Columbia and Ontario were picked in ideal conditions in late December. "We finished picking before New Year's Eve. It was the first time in a while that I was able to enjoy ringing in the New Year without having to look at the thermometer," said Klaus Reif, proprietor and winemaker of Reif Estate Winery in Niagara-on-the-Lake.

According to Winemaster Herbert Konzelmann, whose 2000 Vidal Icewine took the Vines Award, the 2000 vintage was a perfect year for white wine grapes. "The extremely intense fruit flavours of the Vidal Icewine were created through ideal amounts of precipitation and perfect temperatures

FOOD PAIRING SUGGESTIONS
Some people serve Icewine with foie gras, but it is best enjoyed after dinner. Instead

throughout the entire growing season. These special conditions resulted in excellent maturity of the grapes at harvest, which is reflected in the Icewine's full body, intense fruit flavours, and balanced acidity," said Mr. Konzelmann, whose Icewine also won the Inniskillin Trophy for Best Icewine at The 2003 International Wine Challenge, London, England and a gold medal at 2003 InterVin International held in New York City, N.Y.

The 2001 harvest season was not as kind. In both B.C. and Ontario, the harvest dragged well into late winter. A mild winter wreaked havoc on the grapes leaving them exposed for wandering animals and birds. But, when the freeze did finally come, winemakers still managed to craft some special wines.

In 2002 winter came early and most of the wineries in both B.C. and Ontario took advantage by picking in early December 2002. Although there were only a few 2002 Icewine's submitted due to the timing of the tastings, those that were tasted show great promise for another magnificent vintage.

As for the aging capabilities of Icewine — the jury is still out — but generally if the winemaker carefully crafts the wine and hits the balance mark, Icewines can still be works of art after ten years in the cellar. One quick note, unless otherwise specified, the prices quoted are for the traditional 375ml bottle.

Tasting panel: LB, TK, RP, WS, CW

Vidal Icewine

VINES AWARD

Konzelmann Estate Winery 2000 Vidal Icewine
Niagara Peninsula $44.45 (476192)
The grand dame of the tasting, this Icewine has placed Niagara's only lakeshore winery on the international wine map. It's a benchmark beauty with notes of apricot, peaches, and a drizzle of honey. Medium weight, there's a lot of fruit flavours (think baked apple with slices of peach on top). Finely balanced acidity and sugar make for a wonderful wine from start to finish. A truly classy Icewine.

HIGHLY RECOMMENDED

Featherstone Estate Winery 2002 Vidal Icewine
Niagara Peninsula $24.95 200ml
One of Niagara's hottest new wineries, Featherstone has released some wonderful gems in the past two years. This Icewine is a fine example of the attention-to-detail the winery brings to its trade. Key features include pear, honey, lemon, and apricot. The palate is adeptly balanced with just enough acidity to give it a crisp finish. Simply delightful.

Hillebrand Estates 2002 Trius Vidal Icewine
Niagara Peninsula $44.95 (37687)
As the only Niagara winery to produce Icewine continuously since 1983, Hillebrand knows something about making the winter elixir. A paint-by-numbers Vidal Icewine, it features lush notes of pears, apple, apricot, and toffee. Mouthwatering caramel, peach, and apricot flavours with a soft layer of acidity make for a supple, elegant Icewine. Crafted to be enjoyed with a plate of Canadian mild cheeses.

Inniskillin Wines 2002 Vidal Icewine, Oak Aged

Niagara Peninsula $52.95 (55108500)

The 2002 Icewine harvest in Niagara was the best in a decade as grape growers were able to pick the frozen gems in early December. The results are seen and tasted in the 2002 Vidal Icewine from Inniskillin. Notes of mango, apricot, and honey entice the taste buds. On the palate, the tropical fruit is balanced by a core of acidity that dances with the sugar through to the finish. The oak adds a touch of finesse to an already elegant wine. Simply a superb Icewine.

Lailey Vineyard 2002 Vidal Icewine Canadian Oak

Niagara Peninsula $40/ 200 ml

Oak-aged Icewines, like other offbeat Icewines that are Cabernet-based or sparkling, often fall victim to being more of a novelty item than seriously good wines. In this case, the Canadian oak adds some focus and intrigue to the fresh pineapple and peach aromas and flavours. Winemaker Derek Barnett calls this stunning wine his Pina Colada because of its distinct pineapple and coconut notes.

Peller Estates 2002 Andrew Peller Signature Series Vidal Icewine

Niagara Peninsula $60 (981613)

Another charmer from the '02 vintage. The Andrew Peller line of wines are the top tier in the Peller series, and this wine showcases its regal position. The best fruit went into this concentrated, tightly crafted Icewine. Opens with lush notes of honey, peach, and star fruit. Rich, intense fruit flavours of peach, apricot, and honey wash over the palate. Bursts of acidity keep the sweetness in check leaving the tastebuds yearning more.

Reif Estate Winery 2000 Vidal Icewine

Niagara Peninsula $24.95 (544791) 200 ml

One of Canada's most consistent producers of awarding-winning Vidal Icewine, Reif has garnered a collection of international awards. The 2000 offering continues the tradition, as it's a true benchmark Icewine. Enticing notes of toffee, caramel with peach and apricot awaken the senses. Once in the mouth, its lush texture washes the blend of fruit and caramel over the palate towards a long finish. Built with attention to detail, this is a showpiece wine that will impress even the most hardened Icewine critic.

Strewn Winery 2001 Vidal Icewine

Niagara Peninsula $44 (467738)

Winemaker Joe Will has a knack for getting the most out of a vintage. Although 2001 wasn't the best year for Icewine in Ontario, he managed to create a succulent, intense wine. Notes of peach, apricot, toffee, and honey transcend the palate. A bigger wine than most in 2001, it's full of rich fruit flavours. Best enjoyed as a decadent sipper after dinner.

RECOMMENDED

Château des Charmes Wines 2000 Vidal Icewine

Niagara Peninsula $24.95 200ml

As one of Niagara's oldest wineries, Château des Charmes has a formula for crafting award-winning wines. Its Icewine is a perennial spotlight grabber at international competitions. This 2000 features raisin, apricot, and sponge candy along with spicy nutmeg on the palate. Finely balanced, it gives new meaning to sweet.

Crown Bench Estates 2000 Barrel Fermented Vidal Icewine

Niagara Peninsula $49.95

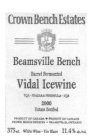

Located on the Beamsville Bench in Niagara, Crown Bench has dabbled in creating some unique variations of Icewine. Yet, when it comes to Vidal, winemaker Peter Kocsis has created a classic. This 2000 includes notes of freshly baked bread with pineapple chunks and peach slices. Lighter on the palate, it has great acidity with splashes of sweetness accenting honey, roasted nut, and tropical fruit flavours.

Hernder Estate Wines 2002 Vidal Icewine

Niagara Peninsula $38.95

Like the move away from over-oaked Chardonnay, lighter styled Icewines are capturing the attention of consumers. This one is definitely light-weight, and there's an abundance of fresh tropical fruit that makes for a special sipper. Lively and crisp, its fruit flavours include pineapple, pear, and apple. A great pre-dinner cocktail served with blue cheese.

Hillebrand Estates 2002 Showcase Vidal

Niagara Peninsula $60 (980144)

Winemaker J.L. Groux continues to show great craftsmanship with his handling of oak aged Icewine. The 2002 opens with an attractive bouquet of fresh peach, apricot, and brown sugar. On the palate, Groux's deft handling of the oak complements the lush fruit flavours giving the wine an added depth and texture. This is an Icewine with style and substance.

Magnotta Winery 2000 Vidal Icewine Merritt Road Vineyard

Niagara Peninsula $27.95

It's a pineapple upside down cake in a bottle. This single vineyard delight leans light on the weight scale, and scores points for its added spicy flavours. A finely crafted Icewine that hits all the right buttons.

Peller Estates 2001 Founder's Series Vidal Icewine

Niagara Peninsula $32.95 (471904)

An approachable Icewine with an affordable price. Fruit characters include pear, pineapple, and honey. Designed as a lighter Icewine, the tropical fruit flavours are highlighted by a crisp streak of acidity. It's a touch of elegance with a splash of chic.

Pillitteri Estates Winery 2001 Vidal Icewine

Niagara Peninsula $34.95 (401448)

As one of Canada's most recognized Icewine producers, Pillitteri has snagged some impressive spots on five-star wine lists around the world. The 2001 is a lively number that hits all the right notes of peach, apricot, and honey. A splash of sweetness on the palate is balanced by a core of acidity. A seamless Icewine for those looking for a touch of elegance to end a wonderful dinner.

Stoney Ridge Estate Winery 1999 Vidal Icewine

Niagara Peninsula $35.95

Although last year's book had this one sliding fast, it appears to have found its second wind. Fragrant notes of rose petal, lime peel, and crème brûlée showcase this aging beauty. Flavours of caramel, toffee, peaches, and apricot are more mellow than younger wines, but a crisp acidity keeps the wine fresh. Some things do get better with age.

QUITE GOOD

Colio Estate Vineyards 2001 CEV
Vidal Icewine
Lake Erie North Shore $41.95 (467472)
A big, chewy Icewine with peach, apricot, and
toffee characters. Its full, lush mouth feel accents
the fruit. Forget the dessert, this is it.

D'Angelo Estate Winery 1998 Vidal Icewine
Lake Erie North Shore $46.50 (554436)
Although there's not many bottles left, this '98 is a
good example of how well Icewine can stand the
test of time. It's highly fragrant with notes of spice
and honey and ginger spice on the palate – it's
almost floral like. It's Viagra for the tastebuds.

Daniel Lenko Estate Winery 2000 Vidal
Icewine
Niagara Peninsula $39.95
Father Time has not been kind to this one.
Showing the signs of age, this one has a deep
melted brown sugar colour. Characters of notes
of tangerine, cinnamon, and caramel weave
through the wine with a tangy finish. Drink now.

Magnotta Winery 2001 Vidal Icewine
Niagara Peninsula $27.95 (486779)
To borrow a line from Sugar Ray Leonard, this one
floats like a butterfly and stings like a bee. It has
notes of honeybee's wax with peach and
pineapple. A little light on the acids, it glides over
the palate taking the fruit with it. Finishes with a
crisp zing.

Mountain Road Wine Company 1999 Vidal Icewine

Niagara Peninsula $34.95

A newbie to the Niagara winery scene, grape grower turned winemaker, Steve Kocsis has his mind set on small batch, high quality wines. Having made a few vintages before swinging open the doors in 2003, this 1999 Icewine has balanced acidity with a rich layer of sweet tropical fruit flavours. Not showing signs of aging, it's a fine start to a new winery.

Riesling Icewine

HIGHLY RECOMMENDED

Cave Spring Cellars 2001 Riesling Icewine

Niagara Peninsula $59.95 (447441)

Another expertly handled Icewine that mirrors the strengths of the 2002 vintage. Features notes of nectarine, honey, and caramel. The flavour profile is an extension of its bouquet with finely traced lines of acidity. Bright, crisp and refreshing, this one should continue to strut its stuff for some time to come.

Cave Spring Cellars 2002 Riesling Icewine

Niagara Peninsula $59.95 (447441)

Considering that Cave Spring winemaker Angelo Pavan has established himself as one of North America's leading Riesling producers, it's only fitting that his Icewine would also rank high. This one opens with hints of stony mineral, lemon, and honey. But, it's on the palate where the wine really shines with its finely balanced acidity and sugar. The perfect blend has resulted in a wine that features lush flavours of lavender, pineapple, and lemon with a viscous texture that provides depth to the wine. This one will age gracefully.

Henry of Pelham Family Estate Winery 2002 Riesling Icewine

Niagara Peninsula $54.95 (430561)

Another consistent producer of finely crafted Riesling Icewine, Henry of Pelham is a sure bet when it comes to this golden elixir. The '02 receives full marks for notes of peach, lemon, honey, and a touch stony mineral. Although there's an ample amount of natural sugar, the acidity manages to keep it from getting too big. Still one of the bigger wines in the tasting, its depth and character make it a fetching wine to savour on its own.

Inniskillin Okanagan Vineyards 2001 Dark Horse Estate Vineyard Riesling Icewine

Okanagan Valley $59.99 (558445)

Although Riesling Icewine is not as widely produced in the Okanagan Valley as it is in Niagara, Inniskillin has continued to nail it year after year. This one has all the markings of a tightly knit Icewine with pineapple, lemon, and a hint of mint. Flavours abound with a good balance between the sugar and acids. Finishes in bright, crisp notes; lip smacking delicious.

Pillitteri Estates Winery 2002 Riesling Icewine

Niagara Peninsula $59.95 (435727)

Kevin Brauch, a.k.a The Thirsty Traveler of the Food Network Canada, features the Pillitteri Icewine 2002 vintage in one of his episodes, and he couldn't have chosen a better vintage. This opulent Riesling opens with notes of sweet lemon, and pineapple with brown sugar. Smooth and silky on the palate, there's enough ripe tropical fruit and acidity to keep it from getting too thick. With a slightly oily texture, this is one Icewine worthy of the spotlight.

RECOMMENDED

Inniskillin Wines 2002 Riesling Icewine
Niagara Peninsula $69.95 (623835)
A tasty Icewine that opens with notes of crème brûlee, pineapple, and pear. Designed to be lighter in style, this is a crisp, racy wine that captures the spirit of the citrus flavours. Just the right amount of natural sweetness make it an ideal partner to a plate of Canadian mild cheese.

Jackson-Triggs Niagara Estate 2001 Proprietors' Grand Reserve Riesling Icewine
Niagara Peninsula $62.95 (593970)
Winemaker Tom Seaver has molded an impressive Icewine from a tough vintage. With a late harvest, he managed to extract as much flavour and acidity as was possible. This one has an intriguing nose of flinty petrol, lemon, and pear. A softer take on Riesling, this one comes across as supple with a tart finish. Chill and serve.

Malivoire Wine Company 2001 Misek Vineyard Riesling Icewine
Niagara Peninsula $36 200ml (591321)
For those familiar with Alsatian Tokai, this one leans towards that style of dessert wine. Golden honey in colour, It features notes of mushroom, apricot, and nectarine. The palate is rich and lush with nectarine and dried raisin flavours. Hints of caramel and ginger on the finish cap an appealing take on Riesling Icewine.

Mission Hill Family Estate Winery 2001 Riesling Icewine
Okanagan Valley $59.90 (624627)
With a difficult Icewine harvest in '01 in the Valley, one in which many producers made Late Harvest out of grapes destined for Icewine, Mission Hill managed to pull off an impressive Riesling Icewine. Intense notes of peach, nectarine, and caramel indicate the length of time the grapes

were left to hang. With flavours of raisin, peach and brown sugar, there's just enough acidity to balance the sweetness. A spicy finish gives the wine an added flare.

Peller Estates 2002 Andrew Peller Signature Series Riesling Icewine
Niagara Peninsula $70 (981175)
Described by one panelist as "spirited," this one is a lean, attractive Icewine that showcases the citrus fruit common to Riesling. Features notes of lemon, honey with crème brûlee, which are mirrored on the palate as well. A lightweight Icewine, this one would be a nice accompaniment to berry tarts or foie gras.

QUITE GOOD

Château des Charmes 2000 Paul Bosc Estate Vineyard Riesling Icewine
Niagara Peninsula $55 (413724)
With notes of petrol and lemon, this one is starting to transform from a fresh to a mellow Icewine. Soft and supple on the palate, there's still enough acidity to even out the sweetness, but it's not as bright as it once was. Finishes on a crisp, tart note.

Quails' Gate Estate Winery 2000 Riesling Icewine
Okanagan Valley $54.99 (539239)
This one is fighting to keeps its youthful exuberance. There are plenty of peach, honey,and caramel flavours, but there's more natural sweetness than acidity and it's starting to show in the wine. Uncork and savour the simple pleasure of a glass of this Icewine and a great book.

Strewn Winery 2000 Riesling Icewine
Niagara Peninsula $68 (554394)
This one is starting to develop some interesting characteristics. Opens with notes of petrol and lemon tea that evolve into canned peach and pineapple flavours. With its soft palate, this is dessert.

Thirty Bench Wines 2000 Riesling Icewine
Niagara Peninsula $35.95 200 ml
Classic honeysuckle, peach, and caramel notes develop into a more citrus-focused palate. Also features generous amounts of acidity and natural sugars, which make it an Icewine that should stand a few more years in the cellar.

OTHER ICEWINES

VINES AWARD

Peller Estates 2002 Andrew Peller Signature Series Cabernet Franc Icewine
Niagara Peninsula $80 (981639)
Hitting the mark with red Icewine is a difficult endeavour, but when it happens, it's special. This Vines Award winner captures the classic notes of Cabernet Franc with succulent notes of raspberry, cassis, and even a touch of green pepper. Juicy red berry flavours combine with finely balanced acidity and natural sweetness make for an opulent Icewine. This is as close as you can get to perfection when it comes to making a red Icewine.

HIGHLY RECOMMENDED

Calona Vineyards 2001 Private Reserve Pinot Noir Icewine

Okanagan Valley $99.99 (725325)

Winemaker Howard Soon was the first winemaker to make a commercially available Pinot Noir Icewine. Building on his first release, this '01 has alluring notes of crème brûlée, orange peel, and strawberry. It's also loaded with strawberry flavours and some spicy notes on the finish. Although a little light in weight, it's a fine Icewine to enjoy on its own.

Cave Spring Cellars 2002 Chenin Blanc Icewine

Niagara Peninsula $59.95 (699231)

Cave Spring has experimented with this grape in the past as a possible Icewine candidate, and it appears that it has passed the grade. The '02 is a lush, succulent wine that displays notes of apricot, peach, and raisin. With its crisp, mouthwatering flavours of fresh peaches and spiced apricot, it has all the markings of a great wine. Simply decadent.

Jackson-Triggs Niagara Estates 2001 Proprietors' Grand Reserve Cabernet France Icewine

Niagara Peninsula $62.95 (593962)

A hedonistic Cabernet Franc Icewine that expresses the tasty red berry fruit of raspberry and strawberry. With a good core of acidity that equals the wine's natural sweetness, it's a tasty treat that looks great in a glass.

Stoney Ridge Estate Winery 1999 Gewürztraminer Icewine

Niagara Peninsula $59.95

This barrel-fermented G-wine has maintained its youthful exuberance. Opens with apricot, lemon, and sugar coated almond. With its bountiful acidity, the flavours of honey, cinnamon and star fruit are still bright and fresh. Leaning on its natural sweetness, it's a more robust Icewine that should age well for a few more years. Drinking well now.

RECOMMENDED

Lakeview Cellars 2001 Gewürztraminer Icewine

Niagara Peninsula $59.95 (590174)

This is a tasty treat that can be best described as a lemon bomb. Starts out with bright, candied lemon notes, which follow through to the palate. Racy and crisp, the acidity really accents the lemon side of the Icewine. Throw it in an ice bucket and serve as an after dinner cocktail.

Jackson-Triggs Niagara Estate 2001 Proprietors' Grand Reserve Gewürztraminer Icewine

Niagara Peninsula $62.95 (593954)

Although Old Man Winter was reluctant to visit Niagara in 2000-01, when he did, those who waited were able rescue the vintage. This one showcases lots of tropical fruit with banana, pineapple, and pear. A little light on the palate, it has a crisp, sharp finish. Drinking well now.

Peninsula Ridge Estate Winery 2001 Cabernet Franc Icewine

Niagara Peninsula $54.95

This is a tasty take on Cabernet Franc Icewine. Appealing to those with a sweet tooth, this red berry wonder is a splashy wine that sticks to the palate. Best enjoyed on its own.

Pillitteri Estate Winery 2001 Chardonnay Icewine

Niagara Peninsula $29.95 200 ml

Looking for a unique spin on Chardonnay? Give this tropical fruit salad a sip. From a difficult vintage comes a spirited Icewine with flavours of pineapple, peach, and banana. With its medium body, there's plenty of sweetness without being too cloying. Closes on a palate-cleansing crisp note.

St. Hubertus Estate Winery 2001 Pinot Blanc Icewine

Okanagan Valley $59.95 (513739)

Pinot Blanc has become a fixture in the Okanagan Valley Icewine market. Like Riesling in Niagara, the grape has proven to be a consistent performer without breaking down. This one features notes and flavours of green apple and grapefruit. Crisp and racy on the palate, it's a concentrated Icewine that is showing well now.

QUITE GOOD

Birchwood Estate Wines 2001 Cabernet Franc Icewine

Niagara Peninsula $65 (637272)

Freshly stewed rhubarb with red berry jam captures the essence of this wine. Good acidity with a tart, crisp finish.

Cilento Wines 2002 Cabernet Sauvignon Icewine

Niagara Peninsula TBA

An interesting take on Cabernet Sauvignon. It's best described as stewed plums. A soft Icewine, it's all about the dark berries.

Harbour Estates Winery 2002 Cabernet Sauvignon Icewine

Niagara Peninsula $59.95 200 ml
Another attempt at Cabernet Sauvignon Icewine. Dark purple in colour, it's a jammy wine that features black currant and plum flavours. Very limited availability.

Inniskillin Wines 2001 Sparkling Vidal Icewine

Niagara Peninsula $69.95 (560367)

Inniskillin is a pioneer of Icewine in Canada, and it's no wonder they were also the first Canadian winery to release a sparkling Icewine. The 2001 vintage features lovely aromas of peaches, nectarine, and pineapple. With its sparkling effervescence, the wine explodes on the palate releasing the lush natural sweetness from the fruit. If the Leafs ever win the Cup, it would be a great reason to pop the cork on this beauty.

Magnotta Winery 2000 Sparkling Cabernet Franc Icewine

Niagara Peninsula $49.95
Taking the sparkling Icewine craze a little further, Magnotta has created a red sparkling Icewine. The first of its kind in Canada, if not the world, this red fizz is full of jammy strawberry and raisin that coat the palate. Full bodied and creamy, this one gets sticky fast, so careful when popping the cork.

LATE HARVEST WINES

When it comes to Canadian dessert wines, Icewine generally hogs all the attention. Why not? It's got a dramatic storyline. Left behind in the vineyard to face an uncertain future, confined to a mesh prison, defenseless against the peril of ravenous birds and the wintry blasts of inclement weather, the frozen grapes are rescued and pressed under the dark of night to produce one of the world's finest wines.

However, that epic tale comes at a price. The late harvest wines produced in Ontario and British Columbia have no such pedigree. But does that mean we should deny them the love and attention they so richly deserve? We think not.

As Canadian vintners continue to experiment with and improve their production of Icewine, that level of knowledge asserts itself with the wineries'

FOOD PAIRING SUGGESTIONS
Remember these wines can be served instead of dessert, as an aperitif or in between courses during a formal dinner. We suggest pairing them with creamy cheeses and a dish of nuts or with fresh fruit desserts that are less sweet than the wine. Salty meats, especially ham or prosciutto, or foie gras would also be a good match for these sweet wines.

late harvest wines, which can range in sugar levels from medium-sweet sippers to I-can't-believe-it's-not-Icewine sweeties (in the case of Special Select Late Harvest wines).

In general, the results of our panel tasting were quite eye opening—as were the prices. Wineries are turning late harvest Riesling and Vidal into sumptuous wines that are perfectly suited to adding some elegance to your next dinner party. Their lighter-bodied style results in a more food-friendly beverage. They can make a big impression without taxing your budget as much as Icewines.

Riesling and Vidal aren't the only grape varieties allowed to stay out late in the vineyards. There were also a few late harvest Gewürztraminer, Chardonnay, Ehrenfelser, Optima and Ortega vintages that ranked high on our scorecards.

Tasting Panel: TK, RP, WS, CW

VINES AWARD

Konzelmann Estate Winery 2000 Vidal Select Late Harvest
Niagara Peninsula $18.95 (409474)
Taking a page from its more glamorous Icewine sister, this 2000 Vidal SLH is simply scrumptious. A lighter version than the 2000 Icewine, it features an attractive core of ripe apricot and peach fruit with a dash of cinnamon. Finely balanced on the palate, the rich fruit carries through to a spicy finish. A classic late harvest that comes at a great price compared to Icewine.

HIGHLY RECOMMENDED

Cave Spring Cellars 2002 Indian Summer Select Late Harvest Riesling

Niagara Peninsula $22 (415901)

Cave Spring's Indian Summer has found its way on to some of New York City's finest restaurants as a unique dessert wine from Canada. Less syrupy than the average Icewine, the strength of this late harvest is in its acidity. Styled after German Auslese, it features pineapple and lemon with a touch of stony mineral. Robust and crisp with a rich core of citrus fruit, this one is built to age gracefully and it's drinking fabulously now.

CAVE SPRING

Indian Summer

2002

RIESLING
VQA NIAGARA PENINSULA VQA
Select Late Harvest

CAVE SPRING CELLARS, JORDAN, ONTARIO, CANADA
WHITE WINE/PRODUCT OF CANADA • VIN BLANC/PRODUIT DU CANADA

12.5% alc./vol.   375 mL

Crown Bench Estates 2000 Livia's Gold Chardonnay

Niagara Peninsula $24.95

This one-of-a-kind late harvest Chardonnay has been made with grapes affected with noble rot (botrytis) giving it an alluring quality. Features luscious fruit flavours of pineapple and banana, and a touch of mint. Soft and supple with a crisp finish, it's simply delicious.

Crown Bench Estates

Beamsville Bench
Livia's Gold
Botrytis Affected Chardonnay
VQA • NIAGARA PENINSULA • VQA
2000
Estate Bottled
PRODUCT OF CANADA • PRODUIT DU CANADA
CROWN BENCH ESTATES • BEAMSVILLE, ONTARIO

375 mL   White Wine • Vin Blanc   9.0% alc/vol.

Quails' Gate Estate Winery 2002 Totally Botrytis Affected Optima

Okanagan Valley $29.99 (390328)

A hybrid cross of Riesling, Sylvaner, and Muller-Thurgau, Optima has been an ideal varietal for producing a succulent wine with grapes affected by noble rot. It has an attractive nose of honeysuckle, lavender, and apricot. The botrytis has given the wine an oily texture that adds depth and complexity to the wine. Like fine silk, it's a beautifully woven wine.

QUAILS'GATE
ESTATE WINERY

2002
TOTALLY
BOTRYTIS AFFECTED
OPTIMA
VQA • OKANAGAN VALLEY • VQA

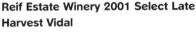

Reif Estate Winery 2001 Select Late Harvest Vidal
Ontario $17 (282855)

With the past successes of Reif's Vidal Icewine on the international scene, it's no surprise its Select Late Harvest Vidal would also receive high marks. Bright and golden in colour, it also has an attractive nose of lemon, apricot ,and peach. Crisp with a delicate layer of sweetness, it's a refreshing late harvest that would be the perfect cap to a wonderful evening.

RECOMMENDED

Gray Monk Estate Winery 2002 Late Harvest Ehrenfelser
Okanagan Valley $13.99 (3211661)

Although a majority of the Canadian late harvest wines come in 375 ml bottles, this late harvest comes in a full 750 ml bottle. Made from the Ehrenfelser grape, it features sweet grapefruit and lemon notes. Loads of citrus on the palate make for a zinger of a wine. A refreshingly crisp and clean wine.

Jackson-Triggs Niagara Estate 2001 Proprietors' Reserve Late Harvest Vidal
Ontario $18.95 (602656)

Another wine that was destined to be an Icewine, but Mother Nature didn't want to co-operate. Opens with notes of pineapple, lemon, bee's wax, and flinty mineral. Feature highlights include: tropical fruit; balanced acidity; and a nice sweet, but crisp finish.

Malivoire Wine Co. 2002 Late Harvest Gewürztraminer

Niagara Peninsula $25

Modeled after an Alsatian Gewürztraminer, this one has attractive aromas of perfumed soap, lilac, and lychee. The palate features a slippery texture with an intensely crisp finish. Flavours include ginger spice and apricot. A great palate cleanser after an evening of spicy foods.

Paradise Ranch 2001 Late Harvest Merlot

Okanagan Valley $29.95 (000034)

One of the only red late harvest wines submitted, the Merlot grapes were destined for an Icewine bottle, but the temperature didn't drop low enough in the Valley before it was harvested. This affordable Late Harvest opens with candied notes of raspberry, plum, and strawberry jam. Dense and full of rich, delicious red berry fruit, it's a wine best enjoyed on its own. The attractive packaging is worth the purchase alone.

Strewn Winery 2001 Botrytis Affected Riesling

Niagara Peninsula $48

Made with grapes affected by noble rot, classic notes of honey, citrus and peach open the wine. Described by a panelist as thick and unctuous, there's plenty of rich fruit on the palate; from noble rot to simply noble.

Thirty Bench Wines 2000 Special Select Late Harvest Riesling

Niagara Peninsula $24.95

Another wine made with grapes affected by botrytis (noble rot). This is a tropical fruit salad of peach and pineapple. It includes candied notes and good lines of acidity with rich, lush fruit flavours. Nice, crisp finish.

QUITE GOOD

Château des Charmes 1999 Late Harvest Riesling

Niagara Peninsula $14.95 (432930)

This wine is showing its age with signs of petrol notes with pineapple and lemon on the nose. With its oily palate and sweet base, it's starting to soften. Best consumed with a plate of mild cheeses.

Colio Estate Vineyards 2001 Late Harvest Vidal

Ontario $9.95 (470369)

Apricot and peach with a touch of honey dominate the wine from start to finish. A tad soft, it's a fine wine to keep in the fridge for nighttime sipping after a day at the office.

Hillebrand Estates Winery 2002 Late Harvest Vidal

Ontario $12.95 (291492)

This barrel-aged LH Vidal is abound with flavours of pear, honey, and hint of vanilla. The oak aging has softened the acidity making for a supple, sweet treat.

Magnotta Winery 2001 Select Late Harvest Vidal

Ontario $14.95

Features lush fruit flavours of ripe peach and apricot with a touch of spicy nutmeg. A syrupy texture coats the palate highlighting the rich, tropical fruit.

Mission Hill Family Estate 2002 Reserve Late Harvest Riesling

Okanagan Valley $34.95 (624619)

An easy drinking Late Harvest with lots of citrus fruit flavours. Soft and supple, it's a charming sipper for those looking for a quick sweet fix.

Mission Hill Family Estate Winery 2002 Reserve Late Harvest Vidal

Okanagan Valley $24.95

Notes of ripe pear and freshly steeped lemon tea give way to a palate filled with lots of lemon. A sweet treat, it's a simple sipper.

Quails' Gate Estate Winery 2001 Select Late Harvest Riesling

Okanagan Valley $19.99 (575472)

Fruit flavours include lemon, peach, and nectarine with a dollop of honey. Leans toward the lighter side of Late Harvest. Drinking well now.

Stoney Ridge Estate Winery 1999 Late Harvest Vidal

Ontario $19.95

This wine is showcasing more floral aromas of honeysuckle with a touch of apricot body soap. An oily texture up front with a crisp mid-palate accent the floral flavours of the wine. Although not a typical Vidal LH, it's tasty all the same.

Strewn Winery 2001 Late Harvest Riesling

Niagara Peninsula $18.95 (467639)

Opens with classic petrol notes with candied lemon and honey. A little soft on the palate, it features lots of citrus fruit. Finishes with a zing.

Vineland Estates Winery 1999 Select Late Harvest Vidal

Ontario $15.99

Features caramel, canned peach, and nutmeg. Starting to show its age, it has developed a soft side that finishes with a slight tartness.

REFERENCE SOURCES FOR CANADIAN WINES

PRINTED RESOURCES

Vintage Canada:
The Complete Guide to Canadian
Wines, 3rd edition
by Tony Aspler
McGraw-Hill Ryerson, 1999

Chardonnay and Friends:
Varietal Wines of British Columbia
by John Schreiner
Orca Book Publishers, 1999

Icewine: The Complete Story
by John Schreiner
Warwick Publications, 2001

Canadian Wine for Dummies
by Tony Aspler and Barbara Leslie
CDG Books Canada, 2000

Touring Niagara's Wine Country
by Linda Bramble
James Lorimer & Co., 2003

Oxford Companion to the Wines
of North America
edited by Bruce Cass, with
consultant editor, Jancis Robinson
Oxford University Press, 2000

PUBLICATIONS

Vines magazine
159 York Street, St. Catharines,
 ON L2R 6E9
Toll-free 1-888-883-3372
Telephone 905-682-4509
www.vinesmag.com
For a free copy of *Vines*, contact us.

BC Wine Trails
P.O. Box 1319, Summerland, BC
 V08 1Z0
Telephone: 250-494-7733
Fax: 250-494-7737
www.bcwine.com/trails

WEB SITES
www.canwine.com
www.vancouver-island-bc.com/
 canadianwines/viwines.htm
www.wineroute.com
www.winesofcanada.com
www.bcwine.com
www.brocku.ca/ccovi
www.agsci.ubc.ca/wine
www.worldsofwine.com
www.gismondi.com

GLOSSARY

Acid/Acidic: Tart, sour or even fresh character, which has an impact on the body, balance and longevity of wine. Generally more obvious in and more descriptive of young white wines, where it gives balance and a crisp, clean taste.

Alcohol: What separates wine from grape juice, alcohol is expressed in per cent by volume of the total liquid and is a key flavour component and preservative. Canadian table wines generally range from ten to fourteen per cent.

Aroma: The range of scents found in a wine, including primary fruit aromas from the grape, secondary aromas from winemaking, and tertiary aromas from bottle aging.

Balance/Balanced: Positive assessment of a wine's character, essentially all of its components (fruit, acid/tannin, and finish) are in harmony.

Barnyard/Farmyard/Stables: Description of a decidedly complex and funky animal aroma found in some red wines. In lay terms could be assessed as smelling of poo, but tasting of heaven. Fear not, these descriptors always sound more off-putting than they actually are.

Barrel/Barriques: Wooden barrels, commonly produced by makers in France, America and, to a smaller degree Hungary and Yugoslavia, are made from oak staves and toasted on the inside for the aging of wine. With a lifespan of four or five years, barrels are expensive (generally $650 to $1,000 per 225 litre (60 gallon) barrel) so are generally used only for wines with the inherent quality for long-term cellaring, a major reason "Barrel Aged," "Barrel Fermented" and "Barrel Reserve" wines cost you more. The newer the barrel the more oak flavouring imparted in the wine.

Barrel Aged: Any wine that was aged in a barrel after the completion of fermentation, anywhere from a few months to several years. Generally, barrel aged wines have more noticeable oak character than barrel fermented wines.

Barrel Fermented: Any wine, though usually exclusive white wine (Chardonnay, Sauvignon Blanc or, in one rare case, Riesling), fermented in oak barrels as opposed to stainless steel or other fermentation tanks. Perhaps surprisingly, although this process adds to the body and mouth-feel, it doesn't necessarily impart oak characteristics to the finished wine.

Blend: A wine that is blended from different grapes, vineyards, wine regions or vintages. It's a case of the sum being better than its parts, different wines mixed together to create the best wine possible. The practice is most transparent in varietal wine such as Cabernet/Merlot or Riesling/Gewürztraminer, however most every wine is a blend.

Body: How the wine feels on the palate, which ranges from light to heavy (or full-bodied).

Botrytis Affected (BA)/Botrytis Cinerea: A beneficial rot that shrivels the grapes and concentrates their flavour, sugar and acidity. Botrytis plays a role in some late harvest wines and Icewines produced in Ontario and British Columbia.

Brix: Term for natural grape sugar, often an indicator of ripeness of the fruit since warmer growing seasons produce higher sugar levels.

Brut: French for dry, used to identify dry sparkling wine.

Buttery: Rich, creamy aroma, flavour and texture associated with malo-lactic fermentation, a winemaking process that converts hard, malic acid (green apple flavours) in wine to soft, lactic acid (rich, butter flavours).

Cedar: Aroma in wine imparted by oak aging.

Character: Distinct attributes of a wine or grape variety.

Closed: Not revealing aromas or flavours. Aging and/or decanting can help it "open up."

Complex: Praiseworthy wine that displays layered aromas, flavours and texture.

Creamy: Description of a wine's mouth-feel, which is akin to cream; doesn't imply lactic flavour.

Cuvé Close: Affordable and fast sparkling wine fermentation technique in which the secondary fermentation is done in a reinforced stainless steel tank; also known as the Charmat process.

Cuvée: Blend of wines from the same region.

Decanting: Simply pouring wine from the bottle to another container in order to aerate the wine and remove sediment, usually reserved exclusively for red wines other than Gamay and Pinot Noir.

Dry: No sugar or residual sweetness remaining (note that a fruity wine can be dry).

Dusty: Refers to the drying effect of tannin in red wine.

Earthy: Describes complex and appealing aromas and flavours such as mushroom, mineral or earth.

Estate Bottled: Labelling prerogative for wineries that grow, vinify and bottle grapes from their own vineyards, generally a sign of quality wine.

Finish: The final flavour impression a wine makes, ranging from short to long duration.

Firm: Describes the texture and structure of a wine, usually young tannic reds that show great potential for the future.

Gamy: Meaty, slightly decaying aromas resembling game meats found in complex reds, another strangely appealing quality given the right dosage.

Grassy: Aromas and flavours of fresh-cut grass or fresh herbs, most descriptive of Sauvignon Blanc.

Green: Unripe, tart flavours and textures usually caused by unripe grapes.

Grip/Gripping: The firmness of tannin (red wine) or acidity (white) on the palate, considered a good indication of a well-made wine.

Herbaceous: A vegetal, grassy, herbal tone in aromas and flavours.

Icewine: Protected term that describes late harvest wines produced from naturally frozen grapes on the vine.

Jammy: Rich, concentrated, semi-sweet fruit character.

Late Harvest: Term with far-reaching application and source of much confusion on wine labels, essentially meaning grapes were left on the vine after normal harvest time. Most late harvest wines enjoy dramatically increased sweetness and flavours, but not all.

Lean: Describes a wine with more acidity than fruit, not necessarily a flaw.

Length/Lingering/Long: Measurement of a wine's final impression after swallowing, following the logic that the longer the finish, the better the wine.

Mellow: Soft, well-balanced wine that lacks intensity, not necessarily a flaw.

Meritage: American term, which rhymes with "heritage" and describes red or white blended wines made in the fashion of Bordeaux, generally a premium wine produced in small batches in better vintages.

Malo-lactic Fermentation: A secondary fermentation, used to soften some Chardonnay and red wines, whereby the malic acid of the wine is converted to lactic acid.

Mouth-feel: Describes the texture of the wine on the palate.

Non-vintage: A wine produced by blending wines from different years, such as sparkling wines designed in a house style that is unchanging from bottle to bottle, year to year.

Nose: The smells and aromas of a wine.

Old Vines: Wine produced from vineyards planted longer than fifteen years ago, the older a vine gets the less fruit it produces, the less fruit on a vine, the more concentrated the flavours, sugars and acidity.

Palate: Overarching term referring to both the wine's flavour and the mechanics of tasting.

Petrol/Kerosene: Pungent yet pleasant gasoline and oil aromas most typical of maturing or mature Riesling.

Racy: Describes lively, zesty acidity, most often found in Riesling and Sauvignon Blanc.

Reserve: Unregulated term that suggests the wine has received much tender loving care from the winemaker—ideally, it highlights a winery's best bottles.

Round: Smooth flavours and texture in a well-balanced wine.

Single Vineyard: Means 100 per cent of the grapes came from the same vineyard, usually an indicator of premium quality.

Smoky: Describes aromas of smoke generally imparted in

the wine via oak aging.

Sur Lie or Sur Lee: French term describing winemaking technique of aging wine on the lees (spent yeast cells) to contribute nutty, yeasty character.

Süssreserve: The winemaker reintroduced some unfermented grape juice into the wine before bottling. It adds some sweetness and can enhance the roundness of the mouth-feel.

Tannin: Drying, astringent texture derived from grapes and barrels, which adds structure to full-bodied red wine.

Tart: Puckering acidity, considered a fault if excessive.

Terroir: A controversial French term suggesting that certain vineyards impart a unique character to the wines they produce which cannot be duplicated anywhere else, with the quality of the soil and the wind, rain and other climatic conditions adding their signature to the finished wine. New World critics dismiss it as a marketing ploy, but a growing number of winemakers are subscribing to the theory, as they identify vineyards that year-in, year-out, produce better fruit and in turn better wine than other sites.

Texture: Overall mouth-feel of the wine, including all components (tannin, acidity, fruit extract and concentration).

Toasty: Pleasant aroma in wine imparted by oak barrels.

Varietal: Wine named after its principal grape, such as Chardonnay or Cabernet Franc. According to the VQA it must contain at least eighty per cent of that grape blended with twenty per cent other accepted varieties.

Vintage: Year in which grapes were harvested; in the case of Icewine production, which often carries over into a new year, the vintage date doesn't roll over.

VQA: Vintners Quality Alliance—winemaking standards, produced and legislated in Ontario and adopted in British Columbia, that cover designated growing regions, grape varieties and accepted practices,

Warm: Describes a wine with noticeable heat from its alcohol content, considered a fault if the perception passes warm to become hot.

Yeasty: Fresh dough/biscuit-like aromas and flavours, more acceptable when found in sparkling wine.

Zesty/Zippy: Describes lively, fresh acidity.

CANADIAN WINERIES

British Columbia

VANCOUVER ISLAND

Alderlea Vineyards
1751 Stamps Rd., RR1, Duncan
T: 250.746.7122
F: 250.746.7122

Blue Grouse Vineyards and Winery
4365 Blue Grouse Rd., Duncan
T: 250.743.3834
F: 250.743.9305
E: skiltz@islandnet.com
www.bluegrousevineyards.com

Chalet Estate Vineyard
11195 Chalet Rd., North Saanich
T: 250.656.2552
F: 250.656.9719
E: chaletestate@shaw.ca
www.chaletestatevineyard.ca

Chateau Wolff
2534 Maxey Rd., Nanaimo
T: 250.753.9669
F: 250.753.0614
E: chateauwolff@shaw.ca

Cherry Point Vineyards
840 Cherry Point Rd., RR3,
    Cobble Hill
T: 250.743.1272
F: 250.743.1059
E: ulrich@islandnet.com
www.cherrypointvineyards.com

Glenterra Vineyards
3897 Cobble Hill Rd., Cobble Hill
T: 250.743.2330
F: 250.743.2496
E: glenterravineyards@shaw.ca

Saturna Vineyards
8 Quarry Rd., Saturna Island
T: 250.539.5139
F: 250.539.5157
E: wine@saturnavineyards.com
www.saturnavineyards.com

Venturi-Schulze Vineyards
4235 Trans Canada Hwy., RR1,
    Cobble Hill
T: 250.743.5630
F: 250.743.5638
E: info@venturischulze.com
www.veturischulze.com

FRASER VALLEY

Blossom Winery
5491 Minoru Blvd., Richmond
T: 604.232.9839
F: 604.323.9836
E: info@blossomwinery.com
www.blossomwinery.com

Domaine de Chaberton Estates
1064 216th St., Langley
T: 1.888.332.9463
F: 604.533.9687
E: info@domainedechaberton.com
www.domainedechaberton.com

Peller Estates
2120 Vitner St., Port Moody
T: 604.937.3411
F: 604.937.5487
E: info@andreswines.com

**Township 7 Vineyards
and Winery**
21152 16th Ave., Langley
T: 604.532.1766
F: 604.532.1752
E: wine@township7.com
www.township7.com

OKANAGAN VALLEY

Arrowleaf Winery
1574 Camp Rd. Lake Country
T: 250.766.2992
F: 250.766.9081
E: arrowleaf@cablelan.net

Benchland Vineyards
170 Upper Bench Rd. South,
Penticton
T: 250.770.1733
F: 250.770.1734
E: benchland@shaw.ca

Black Hill Estate Winery
30880 Black Sage Rd.,
RR1 S52, C22, Oliver
T: 250.498.0666
F: 250.498.0690
E: info@blackhillswinery.com
www.blackhillswinery.com

Blasted Church Winery
368 Parsons Rd., Okanagan Falls
T: 250.497.1125
F: 250.497.1126
E: intrigued@blastedchurch.com

Blue Mountain Vineyard
Allendale Rd., Okanagan Falls
T: 250.497.8244
F: 250.497.6160
E: bluemountain@
    bluemountainwinery.com
www.bluemountainwinery.com

Burrowing Owl Estate Winery
100 Burrowing Owl Place, RR1
S52, C20, Oliver
T: 877.498.6020
F: 250.498.2753
E: info@bovwine.com

Calona Vineyards
1125 Richter St., Kelowna
T: 800.663.5086
F: 250.762.2999
E: wineboutique@cascadia.ca
www.calonavineyards.ca

233

Carriage House Wines
32764 Black Sage Rd., Oliver
T: 250.498.8818
F: 250.498.8818
E: carhsewines@otvcablelan.net

CedarCreek Estate Winery
5445 Lakeshore Rd., Kelowna
T: 800.730.6463
F: 250.764.2603
E: info@cedarcreek.bc.ca
www.cedarcreek.bc.ca

Domaine Combret
32057 Road 13, Oliver
T: 250.498.6966
F: 250.498.8879
E: info@combretwine.com
www.combretwine.com

Fairview Cellars
13147 334th Ave., Oliver
T: 250.498.2211
F: 250.498.2130
E: beggert@img.net

Gehringer Brothers Winery
Rd. 8, RR1, S23, C4, Oliver
T: 250.498.3537
F: 2350.498.3510

Gray Monk Estate Winery
1055 Camp Rd., Okanagan Centre
T: 1.800.663.4205
F: 250.766.3390
E: mailbox@graymonk.com
www.graymonk.com

Hainle Vineyard Estate Winery
5355 Trepanier Bench Rd.,
Peachland
T: 250.767.2525
F: 250.767.2543
E: sandra@hainle.com
www.hainle.com

Hawthorne Mountain Vineyards
Green Lake Rd., Box 480,
Okanagan Falls
T: 250.497.8267
F: 250.497.8073
E: hawthorn@vip.net
www.hmvineyard.com

Hester Creek Estate Winery
13163 326th St., Oliver
T: 250.498.4435
F: 250.498.0651
E: info@hestercreek.com
www.hestercreek.com

Hillside Estate Winery
1350 Naramata Rd., Penticton
T: 1.888.923.9463
F: 250.493.6294
E: klauzon@hillsideestate.com
www.hillsideestate.com

House of Rose Winery
2270 Garner Rd., Kelowna
T: 250.765.0802
F: 250.765.7762
E: arose@shuswap.net

Inniskillin Okanagan Vineyards
Road 11 West, RR1 S24, C5, Oliver
T: 1.800.498.6211
F: 250.498.4566
www.inniskillin.com

Jackson-Triggs Okanagan
Highway 97, PO Box 1650, Oliver
T: 250.498.4981
F: 250.498.6505
www.atlaswine.com

Kettle Valley Winery
2988 Hayman Rd. Naramata
T: 250.496.5898
F: 250.496.5298
E: kettlevalleywinery@telus.net

Lake Breeze Vineyards
930 Sammet Rd.
T: 250.496.5659
F: 250.496.5894
E: lakebreeze@telus.net
www.lakebreezewinery.ca

Lang Vineyards Ltd.
2493 Gammon Rd., Naramata
T: 250.496.5987
F: 250.496.5706
www.langvineyards.com

Larch Hills Winery
110 Timms Rd., Salmon Arm
T: 250.832.0155
F: 250.832.9419
www.larchhillswinery.com

Mission Hill Family Estate
1730 Mission Hill, Westbank
T: 250.768.7611
F: 250.768.2044
E: info@missionhillwinery.com
www.missionhillwinery.com

Mt. Boucherie Estate Winery
829 Douglas Rd., Kelowna
T: 250.769.8803
F: 250.769.9330
E: sales@mtboucherie.bc.ca
www.mtboucherie.bc.ca

Nichol Vineyard
RR1, S14, C13, 1285 Smethurst,
Naramata
T: 250.496.5962
F: 250.496.4275

Nk'Mip Cellars
1400 Rancher Creek Rd.
Osoyoos
T: 250.495.2985
F: 250.495.2986
E: winery@nkmip.ca

Paradise Ranch Vineyards
Naramata Rd., Naramata
T: 604.683.6040
F: 604.683.8611
E: info@icewines.com
www.icewines.com

Pentâge Wines
4400 Lakeside Rd., Penticton
T: 250.493.4008
F: 250.493.4008
E: pentage@vip.net
www.pentage.com

Pinot Reach Cellars
1670 Dehart Rd., Kelowna
T: 250.764.0078
F: 250.764.0771
E: winery@pinotreach.com
www.pinotreach.com

Quails' Gate Estate Winery
3303 Boucherie Rd., Kelowna
T: 250.769.4451
F: 250.769.3451
E: info@quailsgate.com
www.quailsgate.com

Recline Ridge Winery
2640 Skimikin Rd. Tappen
T: 250.835.2212
F: 250.835.2228
E: inquiry@recline-ridge.bc.ca
www.recline-ridge.bc.ca

Red Rooster Winery
910 Debeck Rd., Naramata
T: 250.496.4041
F: 250.496.5674
E: redrooster@img.net
www.redroosterwinery.com

Silver Sage Winery
32032 87th St., Oliver
T: 250.498.0310
E: silversagewinery@hotmail.com

St. Hubertus Estate Winery
5225 Lakeshore Rd., Kelowna
T: 1.800.989.9463
F: 250.764.0499
E: wine@st-hubertus.bc.ca
www.st-hubertus.bc.ca

Stag's Hollow Winery
Sunvalley Way, Okanagan Falls
T: 250.497.6162
F: 250-497-6162
E: stagwine@vip.net

Sumac Ridge Estate Winery
Highway 97, PO Box 307,
Summerland
T: 250.494.0451
F: 250.494.3456
E: sumac@vip.net
www.sumacridge.com

Summerhill Estate Winery
14870 Chute Lake Rd., Kelowna
T: 250.764.8000
F: 250.764.2598
E: info@summerhill.bc.ca
www.summerhill.bc.ca

Thornhaven Estates Winery
6816 Andrew Ave., Summerland
T: 250.494.8683
F: 250.494.8672
E: sales@thornhaven.com
www.thornhaven.com

Tinhorn Creek Vineyards
32830 Tinhorn Creek Rd.,
    PO Box 2010, Oliver
T: 1.888.484.6467
F: 250.498.3228
E: winery@tinhorn.com
www.tinhorn.com

Wild Goose Vineyards
2145 Sun Valley Way,
Okanagan Falls
T: 250.497.8919
F: 250.497.6835
E: info@wildgoosewinery.com
www.wildgoosewinery.com

ONTARIO

NIAGARA PENINSULA

Angels Gate Winery
4260 Mountainview Rd.,
Beamsville
T: 905.563.3942
F: 905.563.4127

Birchwood Estate Winery
4676 Cherry Ave., Vineland
T: 905.562.8463
F: 905.562.6344
E: agreen@diamondwines.com
www.birchwoodwines.com

Caroline Cellars Winery
1028 Line 2, Niagara-on-the-Lake
T: 905.468.8814
F: 905.468.4042
www.lakeitfarms.com

Cave Spring Cellars
3836 Main St., Jordan
T: 905.562.3581
F: 905.562.3232
E: cscwine@cavespringcellars.com
www.cavespringcellars.com

Château des Charmes Winery
1025 York Rd., Niagara-on-the-Lake
T: 905.262.4219
F: 905.262.5548
E: info@chateaudescharmes.com
www.chateaudescharmes.com

Creekside Estate Winery
2170 4th Ave., Jordan Station
T: 1.877.262.9463
F: 905.562.5493
www.creeksideestatewinery.com

Crown Bench Estates Winery
3850 Aberdeen Rd., Beamsville
T: 888.537.6192
F: 905.563.3441
E: winery@crownbenchestates.com
www.crownbenchestates.com

Daniel Lenko Estate Winery
5246 Regional Rd. 81, Beamsville
T: 905.563.7756
F: 905.563.3317
E: oldvines@daniellenko.com
www.daniellenko.com

DeSousa Wine Cellars
3753 Quarry Rd., Beamsville
T: 905.563.7269
F: 905.338.9404
www.desousawines.com

EastDell Estates
4041 Locust Lane, Beamsville
T: 905.563.9463
F: 905.563.1241
E: winery@eastdell.com
www.eastdell.com

Featherstone Estate Winery
3678 Victoria Ave., Vineland
T: 905.562.1949
F: 905.562.3989
www.featherstonewinery.ca

Frog Pond Farm
1385 Larkin Rd, RR 6
T: 905.468.1079
F: 905.468.5665
E: jens@frogpondfarm.ca
www.frogpondfarm.com

Harbour Estates Winery
4362 Jordan Rd., Jordan Station
T: 1.877.439.9463
F: 905.562.3829
E: info@hewwine.com
www.hewwine.com

Harvest Estate Wines
1179 4th Ave., St. Catharines
T: 905.684.3300
E: wine@harvestwines.com
www.harvestwines.com

Henry of Pelham Family Estate Winery
1469 Pelham Rd., St. Catharines
T: 905.684.8423
F: 905.684.8444
E: winery@henryofpelham.com
www.henryofpelham.com

Hernder Estate Winery
1607 8th Ave., St. Catharines
T: 905.684.3300
F: 905.684.3303
E: wine@vaxxine.com
www.hernder.com

Hillebrand Estates
1249 Niagara Stone Rd.,
Highway 55, RR2,
Niagara-on-the-Lake
T: 1.800.582.8412
E: info@hillebrand.com
www.hillebrand.com

Inniskillin Wines
Niagara Parkway at Line 3, RR1,
Niagara-on-the-Lake
T: 905.468.2187
F: 905.468.5355
E: inniskil@inniskillin.com
www.inniskillin.com

Jackson-Triggs Niagara Estates Winery
2145 Highway 55,
Niagara-on-the-Lake
T: 866.569.4637
E: info@jacksontriggswinery.com
www.jacksontriggswinery.com

Joseph's Estate Winery
1811 Niagara Stone Rd.,
Highway 55, RR3,
Niagara-on-the-Lake
T: 905.468.1259
F: 905.468.9242
E: info@josephsestatewines.com
www.josephsestatewines.com

Kacaba Vineyards
3550 King St., Vineland
T: 905.562.5625
F: 416.361.1776
www.kacabavineyards.com

Konzelmann Estate Winery
1096 Lakeshore Rd.,
Niagara-on-the-Lake
T: 905.935.2866
F: 905.935.2864
E: wine@konzelmannwines.com
www.konzelmannwines.com

Lailey Vineyard
15940 Niagara Parkway
Niagara on the Lake
T: 905.468.0503
F: 905.468.8012
www.laileyvineyard.com

Lakeview Cellars Estate Winery
4037 Cherry Ave., Vineland
T: 905.562.5685
F: 905.562.0673
E: lakecell@lakeviewcellars.on.ca
www.lakeviewcellars.on.ca

Legends Estate Winery
4888 Ontario St. North, Beamsville
T: 905.563.5600
F: 905.563.1672
www.legendsestates.com

Magnotta Cellars
4701 Ontario St., Beamsville
T: 905.563.5313
F: 905.738.5551
E: info@magnotta.com
www.magnotta.com

Maleta Vineyards
450 Queenston Rd., RR4,
Niagara-on-the-Lake
T: 605.685.8486
F: 905.685.7998
www.maletaestatewinery.ca

Malivoire Wine Company
4260 King St. E., Regional Rd. 81,
 Beamsville
T: 866.644.2244
F: 905.563.9512
E: order@malivoire.com
www.malivoirewineco.com

Marynissen Estates
RR6, Concession 1,
Niagara-on-the-Lake
T: 905.468.7270
F: 905.468.5784
www.marynissen.com

Mountain Road Wine Company
4016 Mountain Street, Beamsville
T: 905.563.0745
F: 905.563.0650
E: info@mountainroadwine.com
www.mountainroadwine.com

Peller Estates
290 John St. East, Niagara-on-the-
 Lake
T: 1.888.673.5537
F: 905.468.1920
E: info@peller.com
www.peller.com

Estates Winery
5600 King St. W., Regional Rd. 81,
 Beamsville
T: 905.563.0900
F: 905.563.0995
E: info@peninsularidge.com
www.peninsularidge.com

Pillitteri Estate Winery
1696 Highway 55, RR2,
Niagara-on-the-Lake
T: 905.468.3147
F: 905.468.0389
E: winery@pillitteri.com
www.pillitteri.com

Puddicombe Estate Winery
1468 Highway 8, Winona
T: 905.643.1015
F: 905.643.0938
E: info@puddicombearms.com
www.puddicombefarm.com

Reif Estate Winery
15608 Niagara Parkway, RR1,
Niagara-on-the-Lake
T: 905.468.7738
F: 905.468.5878
E: wine@reifwinery.com
www.reifwinery.com

Ridgepoint Wines
3900 Cherry Ave., Vineland
T:905.562.8853
F: 905.562.8854
E: info@ridgepointwines.com
www.ridgepointwines.com

Riverview Cellars
15376 Niagara Parkway, Niagara
  on the Lake
T:905.262.0636
F: 905.262.0462
E: winery@riverviewcellars.com
www.riverviewcellars.com

Rockway Glen Estate Winery
3290 9th St., St. Catharines
T:905.641.5771
F: 905.641.2031
E: rockway@niagara.com
www.rockwayglen.com

Stonechurch Vineyards
1242 Irvine Rd., RR5,
Niagara-on-the-Lake
T: 905.935.3535
F: 905.646.8892
E: wine@stonechurch.com
www.stonechurch.com

Stoney Ridge Estate Winery
3201 King St., Regional Rd. 81,
Vineland
T: 905.562.1324
F: 905.562.7777
www.stoneyridge.com

Strewn Wines
1339 Lakeshore Rd.,
Niagara-on-the-Lake
T: 905.468.1229
F: 905.468.8305
E: info@strewnwinery.com
www.strewnwinery.com

Thirteenth Street Wine Co.
3983 13th St. South, RR1, Jordan
  Station
T: 905.562.9463
F: 905.562.8766
E: funkwine@vaxxine.com
www.13thstreetwines.com

Thirty Bench Wines
4281 Mountainview Rd.,
  Beamsville
T: 905.563.1698
F: 905.563.3921
E: wine@thirtybench.com
www.thirtybench.com

Thomas & Vaughan Vintners
4245 King St., Regional Rd. 81,
   Beamsville
T: 905.563.7737
F: 905.563.4114
E: info@thomasandvaughan.com
www.thomasandvaughan.com

Trillium Hill Estate Winery
34209th St., St. Catharines
T: 905.684.4419
F: 905.684.3911
E: info@trilliumhillwinery.com
www.trilliumhillwinery.com

Vineland Estates Winery
3620 Moyer Rd., RR1, Vineland
T: 905-562.7088
F: 905.562.3071
E: wine@vineland.com
www.vineland.com

Willow Heights Winery
3751 Regional Rd. 81, RR1,
   Vineland
T: 905.562.4945
F: 905.562.5761
E: info@willowheightswinery.com
www.willowheightswinery.com

LAKE ERIE NORTH SHORE

Colio Estate Vineyards
1 Colio Dr., Harrow
T: 1.800.265.1322
F: 519.738.3070
E: cheers@coliowinery.com
www.colio.com

Grape Tree Estate Winery
308 Mersea Rd. 3, Leamington
T: 519.322.2081
F: 519.324.9786
E: winery@grapetreewines.com
www.grapetreewines.com

Pelee Island Winery
455 Seacliff Dr., Kingsville
T: 1.800.597.3533
F: 519.733.6553
E: pelee@peleeisland.com
www.peleeisland.com

TORONTO

Cilento Wines
672 Chrislea Rd., Woodbridge
T: 1.888.245.9463
F: 905.264.8671
E: cilento@ica.net
www.cilento.com

Southbrook Winery
1061 Major Mackenzie Dr., Maple
T: 905.832.2548
F: 905.832.9811
E: office@southbrook.com
www.southbrook.com

INDEX OF WINERIES

INDEX OF WINES

Inniskillin Okanagan Vineyards 2001 Dark Horse Estate Vineyard Riesling Icewine 211
Inniskillin Wines 2000 Chardonnay Founders' Reserve 37
Inniskillin Wines 2002 Pinot Grigio 80
Inniskillin Wines 2002 Late Autumn Riesling 92
Inniskillin Wines 2002 Cabernet Franc 139
Inniskillin Wines 2000 Cabernet-Merlot 160
Inniskillin Winery 2002 Pinot Noir 180
Inniskillin Wines 2000 Brae Burn Estate Shiraz 190
Inniskillin Wines 2002 Vidal Icewine, Oak Aged 203
Inniskillin Wines 2002 Riesling Icewine 212
Inniskillin Wines 2001 Sparkling Vidal Icewine 218

Jackson-Triggs Niagara Estate 2001 Chardonnay Delaine Vineyard 38
Jackson-Triggs Niagara Estate 2001 Chardonnay Proprietors' Grand Reserve 38
Jackson-Triggs Niagara Estate 2002 Proprietors' Reserve Gewürztraminer 58
Jackson-Triggs Niagara Estate 2002 Delaine Vineyard Gewürztraminer 60
Jackson-Triggs Niagara Estate 2001 Delaine Vineyard Riesling 88
Jackson-Triggs Niagara Estate 2002 Riesling Proprietors' Reserve 92
Jackson-Triggs Niagara Estate 2002 Proprietors' Reserve Sauvignon Blanc 102
Jackson-Triggs Niagara Estate 2001 Proprietors' Reserve Méthode Cuve Close 121
Jackson-Triggs Niagara Estate 1999 Proprietors' Grand Reserve Methode Classique 120
Jackson-Triggs Niagara Estate 2001 Delaine Vineyard Cabernet-Merlot 154
Jackson-Triggs Niagara Estate 2001 Delaine Vineyard Merlot 167
Jackson-Triggs Niagara Estate 2001 Delaine Vineyard Pinot Noir 181
Jackson-Triggs Niagara Estate 2001 Proprietors' Grand Reserve Riesling Icewine 212
Jackson-Triggs Niagara Estates 2001 Proprietors' Grand Reserve Cabernet France Icewine 215
Jackson-Triggs Niagara Estate 2001 Proprietors' Grand Reserve Gewürztraminer Icewine 216
Jackson-Triggs Niagara Estate 2001 Proprietors' Reserve Late Harvest Vidal 222
Jackson-Triggs Okanagan Estate 2002 Proprietors' Reserve Gewürztraminer 62,

Jackson-Triggs Okanagan Estate 2002 Dry Riesling 87
Jackson-Triggs Okanagan Estate 2002 Proprietors' Reserve 2002 Sauvignon Blanc 101
Jackson-Triggs Okanagan Estate 2002 Proprietors' Reserve Viognier 108
Jackson-Triggs Okanagan Estate 2001 Proprietors' Grand Reserve Meritage 151
Jackson-Triggs Okanagan Estate 2001 Proprietors' Reserve Meritage 155
Jackson-Triggs Okanagan Estate 2000 Merlot Proprietors' Grand Reserve 165
Jackson-Triggs Okanagan Estate 2001 Proprietors' Reserve Merlot 167
Jackson-Triggs Okanagan Estate 2000 Shiraz Proprietors' Grand Reserve 190

Kacaba Vineyards 2002 Pinot Gris 75
Kacaba Vineyards 2000 Cabernet Sauvignon Barrel Aged 146
Kacaba Vineyards 2000 Meritage 155
Kacaba Vineyards 2000 Cabernet155
Kacaba Vineyards 2000 Pinot Noir 182
Konzelmann Estate Winery 2000 Chardonnay Grand Reserve 42
Konzelmann Estate Winery 2000 Riesling Grand Reserve Classic 88
Konzelmann Estate Winery 2000 Vidal Icewine 204
Konzelmann Estate Winery 2000 Vidal Select Late Harvest 220

Lailey Vineyard 2002 Chardonnay Canadian Oak 38
Lailey Vineyard 2001 Chardonnay Old Vines 42
Lailey Vineyard 2002 Sauvignon Blanc 102
Lailey Vineyards 2002 Vidal 108
Lailey Vineyard 2001 Cabernet Franc 139
Lailey Vineyard 2001 Cabernet Sauvignon 146
Lailey Vineyard 2002 Cabernet-Merlot 156
Lailey Vineyard 2001 Merlot Estate 166
Lailey Vineyard 2002 Vidal Icewine Canadian Oak 205
Lake Breeze Vineyards 2002 Gewürztraminer 66
Lake Breeze Vineyards 2002 Pinot Blanc 70
Lake Breeze Vineyards 2002 Pinot Gris 76

Puddicombe Estate Winery 2001 Riesling Estate Bottled 94

Puddicombe Estate Winery 2001 Sauvignon Blanc 98

Quails' Gate Estate Winery 2001 Chardonnay Family Reserve 41

Quails' Gate Estate Winery 2001 Chardonnay Limited Release 47

Quails' Gate Estate Winery 2002 Allison Ranch Un-Oaked Chardonnay 55

Quails' Gate Estate Winery 2002 Gewürztraminer Limited Release 65

Quails' Gate Estate Winery 2002 Dry Riesling Limited Release 86

Quails' Gate Estate Winery 2002 Riesling Family Reserve 95

Quails' Gate Estate Winery 2002 Fumé Blanc Family Reserve 101

Quails' Gate Estate Winery 2002 Chenin Blanc Family Reserve 107

Quails' Gate Estate Winery 2002 Chenin Blanc 109

Quails' Gate Estate Winery 2002 Chasselas/Pinot Blanc 116

Quails' Gate Estate Winery 2001 Cabernet Sauvignon Limited Edition 148

Quails' Gate Estate Winery 2001 Merlot Limited Release 167

Quails' Gate Estate Winery 2001 Allison Ranch Merlot 170

Quails' Gate Estate Winery 2001 Pinot Noir 178

Quails' Gate Estate Winery 2001 Pinot Noir Family Reserve 180

Quails' Gate Estate Winery 2001 Old Vines Foch Limited Release 198

Quails' Gate Estate Winery 2000 Riesling Icewine 214

Quails' Gate Estate Winery 2002 Totally Botrytis Affected Optima 222

Quails' Gate Estate Winery 2001 Select Late Harvest Riesling 226

Reif Estate Winery 2002 Premium Select Chardonnay 45

Reif Estate Winery 1999 Chardonnay Reserve Estate 51

Reif Estate Winery 2002 Vidal 112

Reif Estate Winery 2002 Trollinger X Riesling 114

Reif Estate Winery 2001 Cabernet Sauvignon Estate 144

Reif Estate Winery 2002 Cabernet-Merlot 158

Reif Estate Winery 2001 Meritage 158

Reif Estate Winery 2001 Merlot 170

Reif Estate Winery 2000 Pinot Noir 180

Reif Estate Winery 2000 Vidal Icewine 207

Reif Estate Winery 2001 Select Late Harvest Vidal 223

Ridgepoint Wines 2002 Off-Dry Riesling 94

Ridgepoint Wines 2002 Riesling 94

St. Hubertus Estate Winery Oak Bay Vineyard 2002 Gewürztraminer 60

St. Hubertus Estate Winery 2001 Riesling 96

St. Hubertus Estate Winery 2002 Chasselas 114

St. Hubertus Estate Winery 2001 Oak Bay Vineyard Chardonnay/Pinot Blanc 117

St. Hubertus Estate Winery 2002 Gamay Noir Rosé 128

St. Hubertus Estate Winery 2000 Oak Bay Vineyard Merlot 172

St. Hubertus Estate Winery 2000 Oak Bay Vineyard Pinot Noir 180

St. Hubertus Estate Winery 2001 Oak Bay Vineyard Gamay Noir186

St. Hubertus Estate Winery 2002 Oak Bay Vineyard Maréchal Foch 198

St. Hubertus Estate Winery 2001 Pinot Blanc Icewine 216

Sandhill Wines 2002 Chardonnay Burrowing Owl Vineyard 51

Sandhill Wines 2002 Pinot Blanc 72

Sandhill Wines 2002 Sauvignon Blanc Burrowing Owl Vineyard 104

Sandhill Wines 2002 Semillon 109

Sandhill Wines 2001 Cabernet Franc Burrowing Owl Vineyard 138

Sandhill Wines 2001 Cabernet-Merlot 162

Sandhill Wines 2001 Merlot Burrowing Owl Vineyard 173

Summerhill Estate Winery 2000 Chardonnay Alchemy 50

Summerhill Estate Winery Pyramid Cellar Aged 2001 Pinot Gris 80

Summerhill Estate Winery 2000 Meritage 158

Summerhill Estate Winery 2000 Pinot Noir 182
Summerhill Estate Winery 2002 Baco Noir 194
Summerhill Estate Winery 2001 Foch Solus
  Enchanted Vines 198
Stonechurch Vineyards 2001 St. David's
  Bench Reserve Chardonnay 52
Stoney Ridge Estate Winery 2002 Bench
  Chardonnay 52
Stoney Ridge Estate Winery 2000 Charlotte's
  Chardonnay Founder's Signature
  Collection Unoaked 54
Stoney Ridge Estate Winery 2002 Pinot
  Grigio 78
Stoney Ridge Estate Winery 2002 Sauvignon
  Blanc 104
Stoney Ridge Estate Winery 2002 Founder's
  Signature Collection Meritage 158
Stoney Ridge Estate Winery 2002 Bench
  Cabernet-Merlot 162
Stoney Ridge Estate Winery 1999 Vidal
  Icewine 209
Stoney Ridge Estate Winery 1999
  Gewürztraminer Icewine 217
Stoney Ridge Estate Winery 1999 Late Harvest
  Vidal 226
Strewn Winery 1999 Terroir Chardonnay
  Strewn Vineyard 44
Strewn Winery 2002 Gewürztraminer 68
Strewn Winery 2000 Terroir
  Gewürztraminer 68
Strewn Winery 2001 Pinot Blanc 72
Strewn Winery. 2002 Sauvignon Blanc 105
Strewn Winery 2001 Two Vines
  Riesling/Gewurztraimer 117
Strewn Winery 2001 Cabernet Franc
  Terroir 136
Strewn Winery 2001 Cabernet Sauvignon 149
Strewn Wines 2001 Terroir Cabernet
  Sauvignon Strewn Vineyard 149
Strewn Winery 2002 Two Vines Cabernet
  Merlot 152
Strewn Winery 2001 Terroir Merlot Strewn
  Vineyard 173
Strewn Winery 2001 Vidal Icewine 207
Strewn Winery 2000 Riesling Icewine 215
Strewn Winery 2001 Botrytis Affected
  Riesling 224
Strewn Winery 2001 Late Harvest Riesling 226
Sumac Ridge Estate Winery 2002 Private

Reserve Gewürztraminer 65
Sumac Ridge Estate Winery 2001
  Pinot Blanc 73
Sumac Ridge Estate Winery 2002 Cellar
  Selection Sauvignon Blanc 102
Sumac Ridge Estate Winery 1999 Steller's Jay
  Brut 121
Sumac Ridge Estate Winery 2002 Okanagan
  Blush 129
Sumac Ridge Estate Winery 2001 Cellar
  Selection Cabernet-Merlot 159
Sumac Ridge Estate Winery 1999 Merlot Black
  Sage Vineyard 167

Thirteenth Street Wine Co. 2001 Sandstone
  Chardonnay Reserve 46
Thirteenth Street Wine Co. 2002 Sandstone
  Chardonnay Musque Estate 55
Thirteenth Street Wine Co. 1999 G.H. Funk
  Vineyards Premier Cuvée 120
Thirteenth Street Wine Co. 1998 G.H. Funk
  Vineyards Premier Cuvée 121
Thirteenth Street Wine Co. G.H. Funk
  Vineyards 2001 Merlot 166
Thirteenth Street Wine Co. 2000 Sandstone
  Gamay Reserve 186
Thirteenth Street Wine Co. 2001 Sandstone
  Gamay Estate 187
Thirteenth Street Wine Co. 2001 Sandstone
  Gamay Reserve 187
Thirty Bench Wines 2000 Benchmark
  Chardonnay Reif Vineyard Estate 37
Thirty Bench Wines 2002 Late Harvest
  Gewürztraminer 62
Thirty Bench Wines 1999 Riesling Limited Yield
  Semi-Sweet 96
Thirty Bench Wines 2000 Benchmark
  Cabernet Franc, Benchmark 141
Thirty Bench Wines 2000 Riesling Icewine 215
Thomas and Vaughan Vintners 2000
  Chardonnay Estate Reserve 46
Thomas and Vaughan Vintners 2002
  Sauvignon Blanc 103
Thomas and Vaughan Vintners 2002 Vidal 114
Thomas and Vaughan Vintners 2000
  Meritage 159
Thomas and Vaughan Vintners 2002 Maréchal
  Foch 197
Thornhaven Estates 2001 Chardonnay 50

A special offer for buying this book

○ YES! Sign me up for a free trial subscription to Vines Magazine. This ballot entitles you to receive two free issues of Vines Magazine! If you like them, you can subscribe at our special rate of $19.95 for 12 issues (two years). That's **60% off the cover price**! If you don't choose to subscribe, simply write "cancel" on the subscription bill, and the free issues will be yours to keep. With no obligation.

name ....

address/apt ....

city/prov./p.code ....

○ From time to time, Vines Publishing allows clients to mail items which we believe to be of interest to our readers. If you wish to be excluded from such mailings please tick this circle

SIGN UP FOR A FREE TRIAL SUBSCRIPTION NOW!

A special offer for buying this book

○ YES! Sign me up for a free trial subscription to Vines Magazine. This ballot entitles you to receive two free issues of Vines Magazine! If you like them, you can subscribe at our special rate of $19.95 for 12 issues (two years). That's **60% off the cover price**! If you don't choose to subscribe, simply write "cancel" on the subscription bill, and the free issues will be yours to keep. With no obligation.

name ....

address/apt ....

city/prov./p.code ....

○ From time to time, Vines Publishing allows clients to mail items which we believe to be of interest to our readers. If you wish to be excluded from such mailings please tick this circle

SIGN UP FOR A FREE TRIAL SUBSCRIPTION NOW!

CANADA POSTES
POST CANADA
Postage paid · Port payé
if mailed in Canada · si posté au Canada
Business Reply Mail · Correspondance-
réponse d'affaires
3873196 **01**

1000060344-L2R6E9-BR01

VINES MAGAZINE
159 YORK ST
ST CATHARINES ON   L2R 9Z9

CANADA POSTES
POST CANADA
Postage paid · Port payé
if mailed in Canada · si posté au Canada
Business Reply Mail · Correspondance-
réponse d'affaires
3873196 **01**

1000060344-L2R6E9-BR01

VINES MAGAZINE
159 YORK ST
ST CATHARINES ON   L2R 9Z9